Raymond Lamont-Brown has written numerous books about Scottish culture and history, including *St Andrews: City by the Northern Sea*, *Fife in History and Legend* and *Villages of Fife*. He lives in Broughty Ferry.

Scottish Folklore

RAYMOND LAMONT-BROWN

BIRLINN

This edition first published in 2024 by
Birlinn Limited
West Newington House
10 Newington Road
Edinburgh
EH9 1QS

www.birlinn.co.uk

ISBN 978 1 78027 847 6

British Library Cataloguing-in-Publication Data
A Catalogue record of this book is available
from the British Library

Designed and typeset by Mark Blackadder

Papers used by Birlinn Ltd are from
well-managed forests and other responsible sources

Printed and bound by Clays Ltd, Elcograf S.p.A.

Contents

Author's note

Much of the material quoted in this book is taken from historical sources and does not reflect modern attitudes and usage. Terms like 'tinkers', for example, have always been used pejoratively, but cannot be avoided in any serious book on folklore and customs.

Introduction

The Boundaries of Scots Folklore Tradition

Scotland is a living museum of folklore. The subject touches everyone, whether they realise it or not, wherever they live. Simple everyday actions, like scanning the sky for rain clouds when there's the car to wash, or avoiding walking under a ladder, can be traced to folkloric roots, or to long-forgotten pagan rituals to appease the quartet of spirits of earth, water, fire and air. However sophisticated we may think ourselves, each person has a race memory of Scotland's folklore roots which may be triggered – at any time – by a thought, dream, an emotion, that cannot be rationalised by modern standards.

In terms of folklore trends, Scotland can be divided into four areas. There's southern Scotland from a line made across Scotland by the old counties of Dunbartonshire, Stirlingshire, Clackmannanshire, Kinross and Fife to the Border with England. Then there's the West Highlands from Bute to Sutherland and the Hebrides. Their neighbour shires to the east – Moray, Nairn, Banff, Aberdeen, Kincardine and Angus – give a different flavour to folkloric belief, while Shetland, Orkney and Caithness, make up the fourth area.

The folkloric personality of southern Scotland was forged in violence and poverty. The idea of a fixed border between England and Scotland was more apparent than real up to the fifteenth century, and then it was only in 1604 that any Border was legally fixed from Lamberton Toll in the east to the Solway Firth. With such a fluid entity the separate monarchs appointed wardens to oversee what they called their Border Marches. Despite the lawful patrols the Reivers held sway. In effect they were plunderers and robbers who exploited the wild 'debatable land' and even harried the sovereign's justice up to the gates of Edinburgh, while defying their counterparts – the cattle freebooters – on the 'English side'.

The frequent outbreaks of dynastic, political and economic disputes between Scotland and England meant that the burghs and abbeys of the Scottish Border were regular targets for pillage. The economy was always under threat and the folk were kept poor as their crops were burned, their craftwork vandalised and their spirit demoralised. When James VI of Scotland disappeared down the road to Greenwich to be King James I of England too, on the death of Elizabeth Tudor in 1603, the poverty-stricken Border lairds in his entourage inspired sneers of Scottish meanness from the English court. When it came to religion, the Borderers had their extremes of faith. The reformed Church was espoused with a will. The independent Borderers were enthusiastic that the new faith said that men and women needed no bejewelled, purple-clad intermediary to speak to God for them, they could do it themselves. For them the Gospels were literal truths, so the spores of bigotry grew large in the Borders, and the witch-hunters' pyres glowed brighter here than in other parts of Scotland.

Thus the fear, anguish, poverty, violence and uncertainty of ancient Border life forged a distinctive folklore. Tales of ogres, witches, romantic heroes, proud citizenry and respect for the supernatural were reflected in the songs, stories and ballads of the makars, the traditional tellers of tales. Still today the Border folklore year reflects the adventures of the Reivers in the Common Ridings from Langholm to the bounds of Berwick-upon-Tweed, and the rituals of half-forgotten pagan ancestors as seen in such festivals as Peebles' Beltane.

The folkloric year of the West Highland counties and islands reflects more the culture of the Celtic peoples, their love of music, dance and games, and their belief in the unearthly; thus there is more than a dash of paganism in folk memory here. Superstition and belief in the spirits of the dead lingered longer in the West Highlands than in Lowland Scotland and somehow the age-old tales of the *seanachaidh* (storyteller) made the folk heroes appear that they lived just yesterday.

Devotion to duty, valour and resilience are a part of the Highland character and the needs of the clan families rose far above individual desires. The clan structure was smashed in the aftermath of the Battle of Culloden in 1746 and in the Clearances – where land-tillers were exiled in favour of sheep farming – yet every year the multiplicity of Highland Games rekindles the folk spirit of the old ways.

Across the Monadhliath Mountains and the Cairngorms to the east, belief in the Devil lingered long, but his dark majesty's minions, the witches, divided into beings that could work both black and white (good) magic. With a long sea coast buffeted by the harsh North Sea, a rich sea-influenced folklore emerged to add a salty tang to the machinations of Satan. Also here memories of pre-Calvinist times lived on.

The far northern islands of Scotland had a different range of influences, as did the Borders. Here the Norsemen ruled from the coming of the Viking longships in the eighth and ninth centuries, to the pawning of Orkney and Shetland by the impoverished King Christian I of Denmark to James III of Scotland in 1468–69. Thus the memories of the Norse gods line up here with the belief of the Picts and the Scots of the south and south-west. It was an area, too, rich in lore of the sea, and all the superstitious rituals that could be enacted to protect the seamen and their families.

The Roots of Scottish Folklore

Generations of Scots lived in that eerie frontier between the mortal and the unseen world that is folklore, and, although exhibiting a Christian veneer, had more than a seasoning of paganism in their makeup, so it is within pagan Scotland that the country had its folklore roots.

Some 10,000 years ago the glaciers of the first Ice Age began to melt and plants started to colonise the land. This evolution was followed by the movement of grazing animals and meat-devouring predators, of which one type was man. Into the land we now know as Scotland, around 9000 BC, people started to migrate from the south and from across the North Sea to till the land. These cultivators of the Middle

Stone Age (*c.*3000 BC) replaced the hunter-fishers of the New Stone Age (*c.*2500 BC) with their axes and polished hammers of stone. In the late Bronze Age, some 3,500 years ago, the descendants of these early peoples were joined in the moorlands and glens by more migrants from the south, identified by their distinctive pots and beakers. They hunted the woods for roe deer and wild boar, beavers, bears and wild cattle. They scoured the skies for great auks, cranes, grouse and the countryside for horses which had come to live here before 4000 BC. From this time the folk began to leave their signatures on rock and cliff in the form of curious cup and ring carvings to mark their passage, or speak perhaps to spirits of their own emergent faiths which they deemed to live thereabouts.

These people began to form centres of mutual habitation on the high hills and built themselves hill-forts from as early as 800 BC, but up to the coming of the Romans these peoples lived largely in individual steadings cultivating land they held in common and retreating only to their forts in time of danger. Amongst this commonalty Scottish folklore began.

The lives of the early inhabitants of Scotland were controlled almost entirely by the powers of nature, and as the actual workings of nature were not scientifically understood, it was presumed by the primitive folk that some supernatural power was at work. To honour these powers upright stones with strange carvings began to appear. Areas of living quarters were cleared and preserved to display offerings to these nature spirits, and even carved proto-gods in the shape of themselves were fashioned by the primitive folk, for the unseen spirits were presumed to have humanoid characteristics.

Modern archaeology has shown that the folklore belief of these early inhabitants of Scotland were divided into two distinct cults to reflect the everyday needs of those who dwelt by the sea and those who dwelt inland. Magic and superstition were first invested by coastal groups in the birds and sea creatures they encountered, and the tools such as shell baskets, fishing lines and harpoons they used to win their daily sustenance. Inland, the animals of field and forest, and the agricultural and hunting tools needed to fill the corn girnels and larder were given supernatural powers. As time went by a primitive pantheon of gods and spirits evolved, each with their own areas of benefice.

The Celts were to be the link between the prehistoric peoples of Scotland and the early historic period in terms of folklore in particular. We know of them from archaeology, oral traditions, Roman writers and etymology, for they left no written records. Coming from southern and south-eastern Europe, the Celts were established in Scotland by the second century BC. Celtic tribes developed their own pantheon of gods, and out of the already established custom of having a tribal shaman they developed their own class of men of religion and learning which the Romans called *Druides* (Druids). The shamans of prehistory, by the by, were usually female, as women with their reproductive capabilities, were deemed closer to the governing spirits. In time this female hierarchy of shamans would lead to women becoming taboo in certain circumstances because of their link with the spirits to form such superstition as it being unlucky for women to board ships.

The Druids, the Romans tell us, living in *nemora alta* (deep groves) and *incolitis locis* (solitary places) and practised their *barbicos ritus* (barbarous rites) and *moremque sinistrum sacrorum* (sinister mode of worship). The Romans also averred that they practised head-hunting and human sacrifices within their *sacellum* (shrines).

Belief as practised by the Celts through their priesthood was based on the nature spirits and sun and seasons worship of their predecessors. The Druids gave to this a new spiritual interpretation through their triple hierarchy of Barda, Vates (seers) and Priests (the *Druides* proper), who acted as teachers, law interpreters and ritualists. Few places in Scotland remember the Druids (*Druidh* in Scots Gaelic) by name, yet here are for instance:

Druig Beg, a loch in South Uist, Outer Hebrides.
Druidsmere, an estate at Blairgowrie, Perthshire.

The Picts enter Scotland's folklore story in 297 AD, when the Roman writer Eumenius comments that the inhabitants of North Britain were known en masse as the *Picti*, the 'painted ones'. They had been around for a long time before that, though, with their origins in central Europe. Together they were to form the major grouping in Scotland of the *Caledonii* and *Maeatae*, forming a definable nation state of Pictland by the seventh century.

Thus was the pattern of tribal scattering and belief as the Romans advanced, by the first century AD, into North Britain. By this time, North Britain could be defined by a rough line drawn from the Cumbrian Mountains to Weardale, and in this land the Romans encountered four partly Celtic tribes called the *Brittones*. In the east coastal area from the Tyne to the Forth were the Votadini, in the west from Ayrshire to Stirlingshire were the Damnonii, in the centre around Roxburghshire and neighbouring lands were the Selgovae and in Galloway were the Novantae. To the north was what the Romans called Alba, the land of the proto-Picts; and all their panoplies of protective spirits and rituals were to be half-remembered for centuries as the basis of Scottish folklore.

The Romans thus encountered an amalgam of spirits and gods of Celtic and Pictish descent in their long presence in Scotland from AD 79 to the third century, and their writers mention the Celtic gods and local spirits of the various tribes.

There was Teutates, the Celtic war god, for instance, whom the Romans compared with Mars, Esus the agriculture god (likened to Ceres) and Taranis god of thunder (teamed with Jupiter). It was the Roman custom, too, to keep an ace up their sleeves in petitioning the *genii loci* ('local gods of the places') and spirits into whose benefice of tribal lands they marched. Thus we have such Roman inscriptions as this left as mementoes by the soldiers; this altar was found at Shirua Farm, Auchandavy, Dumbartonshire:

GENIO TERRAE BRITANNICAE M(ARIUS) COCCEI(US)
FIRMUS C(ENTURIO) LEG(IONIS) II AUG(USTAE)
TO THE GENIUS OF THE LAND OF BRITAIN, MARIUS
COCCEIUS FIRMUS, CENTURION OF THE SECOND
AUGUSTA LEGION (SET THIS UP).

Celtic Gods lent their names to these locations:

Darnaway (from Gaelic *taranaich*), Morayshire, from the God Taranis.

Kyle, Ayrshire, and as a prefix of several places, from Camulos, King of the Tuatha de Donann, a group of Celtic migrants.

Annan, Dumfriesshire, from Anu, mother of the Celtic gods.

Slamannan – 'Moor of Mannan' – Stirlingshire, from Manau, son of the Celtic Sea God Llyr. (See also Clackmannan – 'Stone of Mannan' – the actual stone was set next the burgh tolbooth in 1833).

Three Celtic river goddesses turn up too, in modern river names, the Dee (Deva), the Tay (Tatha) and the Clyde (Clotha). While Angus, son of Dagda, king of the Tuatha de Donnan, has an ancient county name to himself.

With the coming of Christianity the Pictish tribes saw the effect of missionary work started by the evangelists of the Church of Celtic Gaul, St Hilary (*c.*315–68), Bishop of Poitiers, his protégé, St Martin (*c.*316–97), Bishop of Tours, and Martin's own disciple, St Ninian (d.*c.*432), a Briton from the Solway Firth, Bishop of the Northern Britons and Picts. St Ninian founded his monastery at *Candida Casa* ('the white house') at modern Whithorn, Galloway and Christianity spread. The work was carried on by St Patrick (*c.*390–461), claimed for the Scots by a birthplace at Dumbarton. A century later St Columba (b.*c.*521) voyaged to Scotland where he confirmed Picts and Scots of Dalriada (modern Argyll and the neighbouring islands) into the Christian faith. In 563 St Columba landed at Iona to found a monastery from which missionaries fanned out to proselytise the faith. By Columba's death in 597 Christianity was established all over Scotland and for a long time marched alongside the teachings of the Druids and the nature worship of the tribesfolk. And now the folkloric roots of future generations were complete.

A Calendar of Folkloric Festivals

Wherever Christianity appeared in what is now called Scotland, the missionaries grafted the festivals of their church onto already established pagan ones to ensure a continuum of belief. Indeed many of Scotland's pre-Reformation churches are built on the raised pagan ritual sites. One example is the church of Dunino, Fife; in Dunino Den supposed 'Druid stones' have been 'Christianised' by incising crosses on them, representing in reality an early nineteenth-century folly.

Thus there evolved this continuation of folkloric festivals from Celtic to Christian:

CELTIC		NORSE	CHRISTIAN
Imbolc	the feast of the Celtic Spring Goddess (February)		St Bride's Day, 1 February
Beltane	the feast of Bel, Ruler of the Celtic Underworld, and Tin, the Celtic Fire God (Spring equinox, May)		Day of the Holy Cross 3 May
Lugnasad	the feast of Lugh	Midsummer, Day, 24th June	Lammas
Samhuinn	the feast of the dead (Autumn equinox, November)		Harvest Festival
			Hallowmass (Hallowe'en; All Saints' Day 31 October)
		Yule, 25 December – 6 January	Christmas

From these roots, too, the old Scottish Quarter days were evolved, when people paid their rents, were hired and received their quarterly wages:

Candlemas – the Purification of the Blessed Virgin
    Mary – 2 February.
Whitsun – the season of Pentecost (Old Beltane) –
    15 May.
Lammas – 1 August
Martinmas – Old Hallowmass – Feast of St Martin
    of Tours, 11 November.

Three sets of prehistoric folklore roots stand out in particular for festivals in modern Scotland, namely those for Hogmanay, Hallowe'en and the various fire festivals.

Hogmanay – As the last bell of the year tolls in kirk and tolbooth, Scotland settles down to a burly of celebrations that are centuries old. Hogmanay was marked by the Celtic tribes on 1 November, and until 1600 it was celebrated on 25 March. After New Year's Day was fixed at 1 January, which brought it into the Twelve Days of Christmas; so in Presbyterian Scotland New Year's Eve took up the festival of what had been Twelfth Night.

The derivation of Hogmanay is much disputed, but the key to its celebration is the Celtic 'gathering' at tron, or mercat cross; in imitation, of course, of the assembly at sacred grove or standing stone to petition the spirits, and where there would be libations to the spirits, modern Scots offer shortbread, Black Bun and a glass of whisky. These are given the rounds by 'first footing' (the first visitors of the New Year) friends. At one time small gifts were brought to neighbours' houses; a piece of coal (to represent enough heat for the year) and salt to mimic wealth.

Hallowe'en – The Feast of All Saints, leading to All Hallows Day, 31 October–1 November – was the Celtic Feast of the Dead (Samhuinn). It marked the coming of the winter when ritual fires were lit to propitiate the sun and purify the land and its creatures. In Scotland it developed as a feast of witches, and such as the poet Robert Burns (1759–96) made good use of its folklore in his verses. There were all the symbols of pagan feasting in Scotland's Hallowe'en rituals, from divination with nuts to dookin' for apples (apples being sacred to the Druids), and the most potent symbol of all, the turnip lantern – a direct descendant of the pagan fashion of placing skulls of the dead on poles around encampments to drive away evil. Bonfires have been an important element in Scottish feasting for centuries in remembrance of how pagan forefathers lit a blaze on hilltops to encourage the sun to return.

The World of Sacred Stones

Since the beginnings of human activity, rocks and stones have been endued with magic properties. Oaths, vows, petitions and curses have all been supposed to have become more potent if invoked on or near certain stones; indeed in Cromarty there is the *clach an mallachd* ('The Stone of Cursing). Stones were also invested with strange powers. At Yetnasteen, Orkney, the standing stone was deemed to move to Loch of Scockness on New Year's morning to drink. A similar power was invested in the Stone of Quoybune, Birsay, Orkney – at midnight on Hogmanay the stone was seen to walk down to the Loch of Boardhouse to dip its head in the water. To see it was to be struck dead.

Stones set up as totems, markers, memorials and burial mounds in prehistoric times were all supposed to have magic potency by succeeding generations, and, as the reasons for setting up dolmens, menhirs and stone circles were forgotten, the more they were looked upon as magic. Even the ubiquitous Scottish mercat cross – the place of town gatherings for 'tidings of weal and woe' – had its birth in the ancient standing stones.

Each area of Scotland can present examples of ancient stones given magic potency by local inhabitants; here are a few for a flavour of the theme:

Cleat Mound, Westray, Orkney. A quantity of human bones was found here which the local farmer ordered be removed and the stones levelled. Thereafter his household was much disturbed at night by weird sounds and vibrations; the odd happenings ceased as soon as the bones and stones were replaced.

Na Fir Bhreige – 'The False Men' – Blashaval, North Uist. Here three standing stones are pointed out as the last remnants of three men fom Skye who were turned into stone by the spirits for deserting their wives.

Hownam Shearers, Hownam, Roxburgh. Here a ring of two dozen stones is said to represent sinners who reaped their corn on the Sabbath.

Carrag an Tarbert, Gigha and Cara, Argyll. Here at the standing stone the Druids executed wrong-doers, the old folk said.

The Magic Lore of Water, Plants and Trees

Of the quartet of elements – fire, water, earth and air – water retained its magical influence until recent memory. Certain rivers, lochs, pools and burns were all given supernatural potency and, the old folk said, the most magic place of all was a river under a bridge leading to a kirkyard – 'the link over which the living and the dead travelled'.

Water from such sources was used to cure illnesses like epilepsy and erysipelas (a contagious disease of the skin), or to avert the Evil Eye. Thus a whole welter of wells were visited at certain times in Scotland to collect the potent liquid, from Barra's 'Well of Virtues' at Castle Bay, to the well at Tully-belton, near Stanley, Strathtay. Scores of wells were just wishing wells like that at Culloden, Inverness, or St Anthony's Wishing Well below Arthur's Seat, Edinburgh.

The doctrine of plant signatures and life-indices played an important part in Scottish folklore. Signatures associated the physical form of each plant with the disease it was thought to cure: spotted lungwort leaves were thought to resemble human lung tissue and were useful for chest complaints, while the convoluted shell of the walnut, which looked like the surface of the brain, made it efficacious in mental disorders, the superstitious said. As to the life index of a plant or tree, this meant that it foretold the life pattern of its owner. Thus if the plant or tree flourished, so would the family in whose garden or estate it grew, but if it withered so would their fortunes.

Rituals governing the cultivation of plants evolved all over Scotland. For instance it was considered important to trim a hedge from east to west, following the path of the sun. Seeds should be sown under a waxing moon if they were of above-ground plants, and when the moon was waning if of underground plants; the moon drew up seeds needing light and heat and kept safe those of underground habit. In coastal districts of Scotland, seeds must similarly be planted on a rising or falling tide. Scotland, too, had a myriad of superstitions concerning plants. Hedgerow flowers, for instance, especially those of green or yellow, deterred malicious fairies. After a death in the house, windowsill plants must be put into mourning or they too will die. Two flowers on one stalk meant approaching death, and flowers blooming out of season were bad omens.

For a long time the 'Seven Sacred Trees of Celtic Heathendom' were held in superstitious awe. These were the rowan and the holly (whose berries could keep witches away), the mulberry and the yew (which the Druids used for prophecy), the oak and the apple (for longevity and good luck), and the hazel. The latter was the tree of the Celtic fire god (Tin) and was associated with protection against lightning. Hazel nuts too were collected for cures of childhood illnesses.

Thus were plants and trees chosen with great care as family mascots and clan favours. The Clan MacAndrew (Andersons) selected the oak tree, the Macarthurs, laurel, the Maxwells, holly, while the Fergusons sported a thistle on their crest and the pine or poplar on their badge.

Scots Folklore of Birds and Beasts

Scotland's early inhabitants gave equal status to humans and animals. They supposed that other living creatures possessed the same skills and emotions as themselves. Thus animals were given the powers of speech and comprehension of events and were rendered totally anthropomorphic. This faculty was thought to be particularly available to animals at potently ritualistic times like Hallowe'en and especially when one year passed into the next at Hogmanay. Thus in Scottish folk story animals often play an important role in helping the hero and heroine in time of need. In many of Scotland's folktales the dividing line between man and beast virtually disappears, and, in the case of Shetland lore, for instance, folk considered themselves to be descendants of animals. Two creatures in particular present themselves as ancestral lines – seals and merfolk.

In 1895 an old Shetland woman called Baubi Urquhart claimed to be the great-great-granddaughter of a seal, and averred she knew many folks in the villages around who had mermen as ancestors. The mermaids and mermen of international folklore are bewitching beings with fish tails from the waist down. Scotland's merfolk are like this while in the sea, but proffer a competent ambulance when ashore. In Scotland, too, the seal is the folklore root of many Hebridean and Norse legends concerning mermaids, but these may be properly called seal-maids.

Seal-maids came ashore, cast their skins and assumed human form, the old stories relate. Should they lose the skin, they must remain in human form forever. Mermaids (and mermen) are talked of as taking human lovers who must be sworn to secrecy. If that secret is divulged then the mermaid or merman can never return to the deep. Orkney has its own family tree of sea-trows – beautiful sea creatures who could be captured when they cast their scales and taken as spouses. Why do merfolk wish to come ashore? The old folk said they came in search of souls and human emotions.

These mystic sea creatures were not to be confused with the *easg saint* (holy fish); these hazel-nut-eating fish dwelt in wells near churches with overhanging hazel trees. The fish were deemed to have powers of speech at certain times of the year. Their magic also included telling the future. Two such oracular fish were to be found, the gossips said, near Kilmore Church, Lorne, Argyllshire.

The water-horse – a kelpie or a boobrie in Scots folklore – is well attested in Scottish legend. In Lowland tales in particular, the kelpie was a black or grey horse-like creature, with hooves pointing to the rear, which could change its shape on a whim. Its skill was to lure people to their deaths in deep pools and lonely waters. The boobrie was the bird-like shape that could be taken by a kelpie. White mottled boobries were to be found in the sea-lochs and freshwater burns of Argyllshire. The kelpie (and the black water-bull) were said to mate with ordinary horses and cattle; their offspring could never be drowned and were identified by very short ears.

The cat, cow, pig, horse, stag, ram, dog, snake, bear and hare have all played a part in the early folk cults of Scotland as seen in cave and standing stone carvings. Other creatures, too, stand out as having a definite Scottish folklore imagery.

The Scots used to attempt to cure deafness by mixing ants' eggs with onion juice and dropping the brew into the troublesome ear. If a bee flies into the house, a visitor will call, and it is unlucky to drive it out. A bee on one's hand meant receiving some money. One way of ensuring this was to catch the first bee you saw of the season in your purse; the money it contained would then be increased by magic. Because the farmyard rooster crows at dawn with the daily appearance of the sun, the bird has always been associated with magic. In Shetland those who were bent on evil were deemed powerless within the cry of a rooster, the farmyard guardian.

The curlew, called a whaup in Scotland, was said to incorporate a spirit which frequented rooftops at night, waiting to carry off the wicked in its long, narrow beak. It was one of The Seven Whistlers – wandering souls whose cries foretell disaster – listed with the plover, whimbrel, widgeon and other birds of whistling note. Scots soldiers thought that such birds crying out before battle foretold great slaughter. Lapwings were generally disliked too in Scotland because their call was said to resemble the shouted word 'Bewitched', but in Shetland the lark was held in great respect, for the three black spots under its tongue singled it out as a bird of retribution for ill-doing. But in Scotland there were creatures far more curious than these.

The Sphere of Fabulous Beasts

Scotland's earliest folklore tales recount the myths of birds and animals which never had the usual flesh-and-blood birth. Even as late as the fifteenth century, when Pope Pius II visited King James I of Scotland, the cleric was enquiring about the fabulous creature known as the barnacle goose, which was said to live in his majesty's northern realms. In reality these seabirds (*Anser Bernicla*), resembling the common wild goose, were deemed to be born of pinewood wrecks in salt water. Sailors said that the birds developed from a resin coming out of driftwood or the planking of wrecks. This resin formed a shell (like a barnacle) and from this the goose emerged. When feathers were developing the shells split open and the birds fell into the water to be nourished. Others said that barnacle goose trees grew along the shoreline of certain parts of Scotland's coast and when the shells were ripe they dropped into the sea.

The *Direach Ghlinn Eitidh* was a curious one-legged, one-eyed, one-armed animal which was to be found in the Highlands. It was described as a seductive creature that lured the unwary to their deaths.

Thus Scotland evolved its own distinctive fabulous beasts and had little room for such classic beasts as unicorns and dragons, although they did occur in heraldry and, in the case of dragons, in Pictish carvings. Yet perhaps the most talked about folkloric beast of this fabulous genre was the werewolf.

The werewolf – from 'were' the Old English word for man – was the myth behind such character stories as R.L. Stevenson's *Dr Jekyll and Mr Hyde*. Over the years it was a term of reproach in Scotland. It was considered an insult to call anyone a werewolf and in the records of the presbytery of Kelso, under the date 1660, there is a note that one John Brown, a weaver, was admonished for calling a neighbour by such a name. In Scottish folklore history the werewolf story covers everything from witchcraft to the worship of animal spirits, and it is likely to be a memory of the tribal worship of the wolf. By medieval times the folklore had tied itself to an acknowledgement of 'the beast in man' (i.e. his worst nature) and that is where Dr Jeykll and Mr Hyde come in.

The werewolf undoubtedly came to Scotland in the baggage train of Scandinavian myth, as there are traditional tales that Norse kings and chieftains could turn themselves into animals; the process is known as lycanthropy. In Norse mythology Fenris the Wolf was the troublemaker in the Viking Heaven and was deemed a child of the culture hero Loki. So the werewolf became as much a fundamental part of Scottish folklore belief as the seal-folk and the mythical bird-women.

The werewolf legends came into focus in the Christian era's dark centuries of superstition and witch-hunting. The association of the wolf with Satan was inevitable in witch superstition, as lycanthropy was said to be one of the gifts given by the Devil to his minions. Ideas about werewolves persisted longer in the Highlands, as wolves probably died out in the Lowlands by the thirteenth century.

Highland folktale is full of stories of wolves attacking deer. The tribesmen of the Highlands, too, would have the tradition of the wolf-cult which was passed down to the emergent clans. Incidentally, any place name with Lorn in it is likely to have an association with the old wolf beliefs. It is taken from the Gaelic *loarn* (wolf) and is to be found in the name Lorn in Argyll, by Loch Leven and Loch Awe.

The witch-obsessed King James VI & I was a firm believer in lycanthropy and people actually made potions of poppy, belladonna and datura for the purpose of turning themselves into wolves through some nonsense ritual. All this stemmed from the old idea of the early Scots tribesmen that if they put on an animal's skin they would take on the character of that animal.

The old folklore tales are pretty uniform when they say what a werewolf looked like. They were part human, part wolf and people believed that they could spot anyone who had werewolf potential. Identiying signs were supposed to be extreme hairiness, straight eyebrows meeting over the nose, strong and claw-like fingernails, small flat ears, and the third finger of each hand being at least as long as the second.

People believed that as werewolves were not spirits that

they could be killed and at the point of death they returned to human form. From this idea stemmed all the folk stories of hunters wounding a werewolf to later learn that some local person had suffered an injury in the same part of the anatomy. Only a silver bullet was thought fatal.

In Scotland it was believed that foxes were the direct descendants of wolves, so when wolves died out, foxes took on the wolf-lore. It was said that the tongue of a wolf or fox made a good amulet for the healing of gashes caused by thorns, while such a tongue boiled would give courage when eaten. Another important amulet was to carry a pierced wolf's tooth, but it was considered unlucky to bring foxgloves into the house. Many folk also associated wolves with weather-lore. Here are some old sayings on the subject:

When the wind whistles … a wolf is sharpening its teeth.
A destructive wind … the wolf's wind.
Sun shining when it is raining … a wolf's wedding
*   taking place.*
Woolly clouds … today like sheep, tomorrow wolves.

Tradition has it that the wolf was exterminated in Scotland in 1650 by Sir Ewen Cameron of Lochiel, but there is some evidence that wolves still existed in Scotland until the 1740s. In fact the date 1743 is given as the year when the last wolf was killed by a deer-stalker called Macqueen in the Forest of Darnaway at the behest of the laird of Macintosh.

As well as for werewolves, a definite folklore developed in Scotland for giants and fairies.

Land of the Giants

Scotland's giants were not known for their good reputation. For this we must censure the Celtic bards, who made them greedy, boastful, brutish and with a penchant for human flesh.

All over Scotland there are archaeological relics like standing stones, long burial barrows and cairns, and natural phenomena like rocks and crags in the shapes of chairs, desks and tables that were considered to be the artefacts of a vanished race of giants who were thought to have dwelt in certain localities. Indeed the tales may have been Scotland's answer to the cosmogonic cycles – the creation of myths of tribal times – in which immense primordial beings were considered to have created the universe. The finding of large animal bones, too, in these early burial sites led to the belief in a forerunning race of giant ancestors.

Distinctively Scotland offers giants of the Gaelic-speaking area, known as *Famhairean* (Fomorians). They are believed to dwell in hills, mountains, caves, sea fastnesses and island strongholds. Then there are the giants of the more lowland mountains, who are usually grouped in pairs of deadly rivals throwing things at each other in eternal strife. Thus in Gaelic heathendom the giants of Munlochy Bay, Ross & Cromarty, assail each other with battle-axes from adjacent headlands. Inverness can offer a trio of giants on the Hills of Torvean, Dunain and Craig Phadrick, hefting stone hammers to one another from dawn to midday. The ice-carried boulders of previous ages standing stark in fields are said to be these hurling giants' near-misses and are so labelled from Banffshire to Fife, and from Morayshire to the Lothians. The strongest of Scotland's giants is identified at Ben Ledi, Callander, south-west Perthshire. He is dubbed Samson and his 'putting stone' is to be seen on the eastern slops of the Ben. Iron Age hill-forts, also, are often claimed to be giants' houses.

Some folktales equate giants with the Devil. Thus the giant of Norman's Law, Fife, is the 'Earl of Hell' himself. He hurled a boulder across the Tay against the Law Hill, Dundee; it fell short and rests today for all to see as a relic of Scotland's mystic past. In time great heroes of Scottish history took on the appurtenances of giants. Thus the Giant of Eildon Hill, Roxburghshire, and that of the islet of Easdale, Oban, is named for the Scottish patriot Sir William Wallace (*c.*1274–1305). Every bard would give his audience an ace up the sleeve when dealing with giants, for it was long known in Scotland that a giant could be overcome at his or her weakest spot, and that was marked by a mole somewhere on their vast bodies.

Equal opportunities are alive and well in Scottish giant-lore, for the country sports a score of giantesses from she of the parish of Edderton, Ross & Cromarty, who flung the spindle across the Dornoch Firth, to the *Clashnichd Aulnain* of Craig-Aulnain, Strathdon, Banffshire. A race memory of forgotten goddesses may be extant in Scotland's stories of female giants, especially those known in Gaelic as *Cailleach* (old wife). A famous reference is the *Cailleach Bheur* who could change from termagant harridan to a voluptuous maiden, and from flesh to stone at will. These were also the attributes of the Cailleach of Ben Nevis. Certain landmarks in Scotland still have the prefix 'giant'; here are a few examples:

Giant's Chair – Dullane Water, east of
   Ballindalloch, Banffshire.
Giant's Cave – Tail Burn, North-east Moffat,
   Dumfriesshire.
Giant's Graves – Northmaven and Stanstig,
   Shetland; Uagh am Fhamhair, Colonsay;
   Kilchoman, Argyll; Enochdow, Perthshire.
Giant's Leg – Bressay Island, Shetland.
Giant's Steps – at the Falls of Tummel, Pitlochry,
   Perthshire.
Giant's Stones – south-west at Tweedsmuir
   Church, Peebleshire.
Giant's Dyke – a hill-fort at Tongland,
   Kirkcudbrightshire.
Giant's Cairns – Old Deer, Aberdeenshire.

Many of Scotland's ancient standing stones have related giant stories. The Callanish stones of Uig, Lewis, are talked about in some old tales as being giants which St Kiaran turned to stone for disobedience to the tenets of Christianity.

The Realm of Elfhame

As with so many aspects of folklore, Scotland's fairylore differs between Lowlands and Highlands, and fairylore is richer in its relics in the former. Only in the Lowlands are there to be found tales of a Fairy Queen, or Queen of Elfhame, the kingdom of the fairies. The fairylore of the Scottish Borders is mainly the relics of folktales of the people of the southern tribes and are classed by folklorists as elves – diminutive humanoids. While in the Highlands fairies owe their origins amongst the Scandinavian dwarves – trolls (trowes in Orkney and Shetland) – and the kobolds and hob-goblins of Northern European folklore.

The Highland fairies had their kingdom 'to the westward' and travelled in whirlwinds and it was by using the power of the four winds that fairies carried people off to, maybe, remote islands or the summits of distant hills. In Gaeldom you were deemed to be able to arrest such kidnappings by throwing your hat into the air and shouting *Is leatsa so; is leamsa sin* (This is yours; this is mine); thus the fairies would abandon their burden. The kidnapping aspects of fairylore have obviously some relic memory of tribal sacrifice as does another fairy superstition – that of the Changeling. The early tribes of Scotland had the custom of kidnapping the children of their enemies and leaving sickly ones in their places; the relic folk memory gave this action to the fairies.

Scots fairies in general were deemed a part of a nether-world that could be arrived at through mounds, mountains, or lochs. All of nature was the domain of the fairies who culled dead plants and animals to recycle them or protect them in the changing of the seasons. Thus was the cuckoo called *eun sith* (supernatural bird) in Gaelic as it was supposed to dwell in the netherworld in winter. A whole range of flora and fauna were given to the fairies by superstitious benefice from blue-bells to deer, 'the cattle of the fairies'.

To appease the wrath of the fairies, who might be consid-ered to have sent plague or mischief to a village, offerings of oatmeal and milk were supposed efficacious. To those they favoured the fairies gave secrets of their own skills as music-ians, craftsfolk, panners of gold, necromancers and concocters of potions for wel and woe.

As to the origins of fairies, folklorists and anthropologists point to their description as 'wee folk' as a clue, and they relate the size to a folk memory of the small-stature peoples of the Neolithic and Bronze Ages, a time range of 2300–500 BC.

All over Scotland there are place-names incorporating references to fairies. The dwellers of the defined 'fairy knolls' (or knowes) of the Highlands are usually female in aspect, described as fair, pale, long-faced and with 'red-gold' hair, while those of the Lowlands are distinctively darker and male. The colourings are to be seen as those of the early tribes of the regions. All fairies are invisible at will. Here are some sites related to fairylore:

Fairy Hillocks – Gamrie and Kennethmont, Aberdeen; Halkirk, Caithness; Wick, Caithness; the *Cnoc an t-Suidhe* is at Kilfinichen and Kilvickeon, Mull.

Fairy Bridge – Dunvegan, Skye.

Fairy Castle – the *Tor Ban Na Gruagaich* (Fairy castle of the Maidens) at Halkirk, Caithness.

Fort of the Fairies – the *Dun an t-Sithean,* Tiree.

Fairy Places – Sithean at Strath, Skye; Oronsay; Blair Atholl and Kilspindie, Perthshire; *Sithean na h-Iolaire* (Fairy Knowe of the Eagle), Uig, Lewis.

Sithean an Altair (Fairy Knowe of the Altar), North Uist.

Sithean Nan Cailleach – (Fairy Knowe of the Old Woman), Eigg.

Sithean Duch (Black fairy Knowe) – Reay, Caithness.

Da Sithean (Two Folk Knowes) – Tiree.

Two Scottish folk heroes are given definite links with fairy-lore, namely Thomas the Rhymer and King Arthur.

Thomas of Ercildoun: Thomas the Rhymer

There is no more tenacious character of Scottish myth and legend than Thomas the Rhymer, made famous for generations in the traditional poem titivated by Sir Walter Scott for his *Minstrelsy of the Scottish Border* (1802). It begins:

> *True Thomas lay on Huntlie Bank:*
> *A ferlie he spied wi' his e'e;*   wonder/eye
> *And there he saw a lady bright*
> *Coming riding down by the Eildon Tree.*
>
> *Her skirt was o' the grass-green silk,*
> *Her mantle o' the velvet fine,*
> *At ilka tett o' her horse's mane*   tuft
> *Hung fifty siller bells and nine*   silver
>
> *True Thomas he pulled aff his cap,*
> *And louted low down to his knee*   bowed
> *'All hail, thou mighty Queen of Heaven!*
> *for they peer on earth I never did see.'*
>
> *'Oh no, Oh no, Thomas,' she said,*
> *'That name does not belang to me;*
> *I am but the Queen of fair Elfland,*
> *That am hither come to visit thee.'*

In Border dialect Thomas of Ercildoun (Earlston) is called 'True', in allusion to his supposed accuracy as a seer. Huntlie Bank, Rhymer's Glen near Darnick, Roxburghshire, is within the estates of Sir Walter Scott's home at Abbotsford. In the story Thomas falls asleep and in a dream state dwells with the Queen of Elfland for seven years.

Thomas awoke again on Huntlie Bank as if he had just been in a short reverie. When he woke he saw a knight in armour. This knight told him he would see three future tragic events – the death of Alexander III (who fell off the cliffs at Pettycur Bay, Kinghorn, Fife, in 1286); Flodden (the defeat of the Scots army of James IV on 9 September 1513); and the Battle of Pinkie (the disastrous Battle of Carberry Hill which saw the defeat of the supporters of Mary, Queen of Scots, in June 1567). To make up for these melancholy visions Thomas asked the knight to show him some blessings. The poem goes on to interlard tales of King Arthur and prophecy.

Undoubtedly in the traditional poem we have the life story of a real person, utilising biographical gaps in that person's actual recorded story to recount supernatural events. Legend tells us that Thomas the Rhymer was a Lauderdale laird named Sir Thomas Learmonth of Ercildoun. He is mentioned in the records of the Trinitarian monks of Soutra as having lands in what we now know as Earlston, Berwickshire. He was probably a vassal of the powerful Earl of Dunbar and March. It is possible, too, that he died at the Trinitarian monastery of Failford, near Tarbolton, Ayrshire. We know that Sir Thomas's son gave lands to the clergy of Soutra (maybe to pay for his father's sustenance and accommodation). At the end of his life it seems that Sir Thomas had a price on his head for having fallen foul of the 7th Earl of Dunbar. He lived from approximately 1200 to 1297 and everything else about him is just myth, particularly him being known as a seer. Thus we have a real person plucked out of the chronicles of history to be given a supernatural role in legendary Elfland.

In recent folkloric scholarship it has been suggested that Thomas was an illegitimate offspring of the Cospatrick Earls of Dunbar. He must have had some influence because the earls would not have let him live so close to their lands in a strong castle. A fragment of what is known as the Rhymer's Tower can be seen between the Leader Water and the town of Earlston, Berwickshire, as the traveller goes down the A68. The extant tower, however is not as old as any that could have been built by a thirteenth-century nobleman, but it may be on the site of Thomas's fortress.

There are those who aver that Thomas had a connection with the Cospatrick Dunbars through his wife. They say she was a daughter of the Dunbars, married unsuitably to Thomas with whom she had to elope. Was she indeed the inspiration for the Queen of Elfland? It is also curious that Forvie, Fyvie and Inverugie, Aberdeenshire, appear in rhymes associated with Thomas. Did he spend some time there, escaping perhaps from the Earl of Dunbar's men in pursuit of his kinswoman? This would mean that Thomas was absent from the Borders. Did local folklore account for him being missing with his Dunbar wife as a basis for his seven years with the Queen of Elfland?

History has Thomas the Rhymer as the author of a story *The Roman of Sir Tristram.* This is the long tale of Tristram de Lyones and the Lady Isolde. The reputed Thomas edition is the first version in English, probably from a French source. The love story of Tristram and Isolde is much older than that of Arthur and Guinevere and because of this Thomas is considered to be Scotland's first major poet.

Scottish folklore tracts are rich with Thomas the Rhymer's prophecies. Yet as they did not appear in literary form until the fifteenth century, their provenance is somewhat doubtful. Here are a few examples of his prognostic couplets:

When Tweed and Powsail meet at Merlin's Grave
England and Scotland shall one monarch have.

(Merlin's Grave is placed at Drumelzier, south-west of Peebles. Local legend has it that on the day of James VI's accession to the English throne as James I – 24 March 1603 – the Tweed overflowed into the Powsail Burn).

Tide, Tide, what'er betide
There'll aye be Haigs at Bemersyde.

(This refers to the Old House of Bemersyde, near Melrose, and the occupancy of the Haig family. Best remembered is Field-Marshall the Earl Haig of Bemersyde).

Thomas's prophecies were widely believed and were the daily conversation gambits in the court and great halls of Scotland for centuries; they were particularly popular during the reigns of James V, Mary, Queen of Scots, and James VI, in the period 1513–1625. He was quoted, too, in the writings of such famous historians as Archbishop Spottiswoode and John Barbour, Archdeacon of St Machar's, Aberdeen.

Yet for all this Thomas the Rhymer is most traditionally entwined with Scotland's fairylore and the other named folklore hero, King Arthur.

Some folklorists believe that King Arthur once lived and fought in Scotland. Arthurian tales were well known in Scotland in the fourteenth and fifteenth centuries. Sir David Lindsay noted in his *The Dream* that he entertained young King James V 'with antique stories and deidis martiall' of Arthur. The best-known version of Arthur's story is *Le Morte d'Arthur*, written by Sir Thomas Malory and published in 1485.

In the Malory version, Arthur becomes king by drawing a magic sword out of an anvil, which no other man could do. Guided by Merlin the magician, Arthur subdued all his enemies to rule in glory. Later he was given his famed sword Excalibur, Rone his spear, Pridwin his shield and Cavall his dog. He married Guinevere and set up court at Camelot. There, too, Arthur established the Order of the Round Table – an order of knights who vowed to live nobly and fight valiantly – but overshadowing this picture of prosperity and honour is Merlin's prophecy of the evil days ahead. The seeds of disaster are present in Mordred, Duke of Cornwall, who Malory refers to as Arthur's son, fathered in an incestuous affair with his half-sister Morgan le Fay, and the secret passion of Sir Launcelot, Arthur's trusted friend, for Guinevere.

Arthur's glory grows for a while, culminating in his defeat of the Romans and being crowned emperor by the pope – but the years of peace do not last. The affair between Launcelot and Guinevere is discovered by Mordred who exploits the scandal to start civil war. Arthur defeats Mordred in personal combat at the Battle of Camelon (which some sources identify near Falkirk), but Arthur is mortally wounded. Sorrowing women carry Arthur to a barge, which sets sail west to Avalon and into legend. Meanwhile too, the knights have ridden out in quest of the Holy Grail – the sacred Chalice of the Last Supper (the symbol of perfection), which Pontius Pilate gave to St Joseph of Arimathea and in which drops of Christ's blood were collected at the crucifixion.

In Scottish folklore the elemental story threads of Arthur, Merlin, Guinevere and the Knights appear. By the twelfth century, stories of Arthur's deeds were recounted in Scottish halls and firesides. Arthur does appear in Celtic legend as a great hero, violent and boisterous, who rid the land of giants, monsters and witches. With his legends are intertwined stories of Celtic gods like Gwynn mac Nudd (another name for the river god Ludd).

Today folklorists and historians say that Arthur was more probably a general rather than a king. Possibly he was a Celtic cavalry leader with a swift-moving force, which would account for his ability to range up and down the country to achieve the dozen or so victories with which he is credited, so the assertion that Arthur subdued the heathen in Shetland, as stated by the monk Geoffrey of Monmouth in *Historia Regnum Britanniae*, is not as incredible as it first sounds.

Legend associated Arthur with Dumbarton Rock and avers that one of Arthur's battles were fought in Glen Douglas on Loch Lomondside. The Campbells claimed descent from Arthur through a purported son, Smerevie Mhor, born at the Red Hall of Dumbarton. One of the buildings of the medieval castle of Dumbarton was called the Red Tower. Certainly long into the fifteenth century Dumbarton was referred to as Arthur's Castle.

If we look at some of the old names mentioned in the Arthurian legends we can see some Scottish references:

Regio Linnius – Lennox, at Dumbarton; Stirling; Perthshire and Renfrewshire; also a Stewart earldom.
Fluvius Dubglas – Douglas Water, Lanark.
Mount Agred – the old Welsh name for Edinburgh.

Then there are these sites associated with Arthur:

Arthur's Seat – at Moffat, Dumfriesshire; Edinburgh; Dunbarrow Hill, Angus; Dumbarton.
Beinn Artair – The Cobbler, head of Loch Long.
Aghaidh Artair – 'Arthur's Face', west Glen Kinglas, Argyll.

Sruth Artair – Struarthour, Glassary, Argyll.
Arthur Stone – Coupar Angus.
Arthouriscairne – Bennachie, Aberdeenshire.
Suidhe Artair – Glenlivet, Banffshire.
Arthur's Oven – Furnus Arthati, Stenhousemuir,
    Stirlingshire.
Arthur's Fountain – Crawford, Lanarkshire.

These are the other characters of Arthurian tale especially mentioned, too, in Scottish folklore:

SIR GAWAIN: the courteous knight, Arthur's nephew.
    Identified as King of Galloway. This region of
    Scotland was inhabited by a race of Celtic Gauls.
    In reality maybe Gawain was a local chieftain.
    The last chieftain of Galloway died in 1234.
MERLIN: The so-called magician of Arthurian legend.
    He is associated with the Caledonian forests and
    the Eildon Hills. His grave is said to be at
    Drumelzier, Peeblesshire.
GUINEVERE: Arthur's wife is associated with local
    folklore with Meigle, Angus. In the churchyard
    there are more than twenty sculptured stones of
    the Celtic Christian period and they form one of
    the most notable assemblages of Dark Age
    sculpture in Western Europe. The stones are said
    to mark the grave of Guinevere, and the folklore
    further claims that Arthur imprisoned Guinevere
    at nearby Barry Hill Fort for her dalliance with
    Launcelot.

Demons, Spirits and Ghosts

When the early Christian missionaries came to Scotland they found a land they deemed full of spirits and demons. The Irish saint Adamnan (*c.*625–704), Abbot of Iona, tells us so in his *Life of Saint Columba*.

Adamnan recorded that one day St Columba (*c.*521–97), 'Missionary of the Picts, Scots and Northern English', was accosted by a young man carrying a pail of new milk. The youth asked the saint to bless him and the milk. Columba did so and the lid of the pail flew off and the milk was spilled. The saint explained to the youth that he had forgotten to banish the demon that lived in every receptacle and dark place by making the sign of the cross. Columba then blessed the pail which was at one refilled with milk. The most famous demon quelled by Columba, of course, was the one in Loch Ness, and Adamnan's story of this remained until the Victorians refashioned it into the Monster of Loch Ness. Loch Ness is not the only water haunted by riverine demons. Loch Morar, Lochaber – Scotland's deepest loch – is the home of the monster Morag, who is only likely to appear to give warning of death of the chief of the Macdonalds.

In Scotland denizens of the supernatural world could take on various forms. The most versatile is the *bochdan*, a creature that could be demon, or spirit, or ghost at will. Its dexterity in appearing as a he-goat, or a grey dog, or a one-eyed monster was famous in a country where spirits are as common as blades of grass.

Evil spirits were always well represented in the *baobhan sith*. They usually hunted mischief in huddles as crows or bevies of beautiful girls with long green dresses to hide their cloven hooves. They were said to lure young men and suck their blood as Scotland's folkloric rival to the European vampire.

There were, of course, hosts of water spirits in Scotland, as well as the kelpie. The Cuchag River Spirit lived at Glen Cuaich, Inverness, and was shunned, as was the malignant, green-dressed *fuath* with its webbed feet, yellow hair and distinctive single nostril. Such a beast was the Fuath of Loch na Fideil at Gairloch, Ross & Cromarty, which hunted the huntsmen who were foolish enough to stray into its territory.

The Celtic *bargvest* lived long in folklore memory too. Eyes like smouldering embers would observe all who approached, yet, despite its claws, horns and devilish tail, this spirit was not a predator – its clanking girdle of iron chain usually gave away its position anyway. It was a spirit of ill-omen whose presence in the fishing communities of north and east

Scotland foretold imminent death. Such was the role, too, of perhaps the most famous spirit in Scottish folklore, the *bean shith*, or banshee. Bynamed 'The Washer of the Clothes of the Dead', with its perpetually weeping red eyes, the banshee would wail the name of the person whose clothes it was washing when encountered, and those who witnessed its work were given three wishes. Usually the banshee is considered female and some stories relate how it married mortals.

As with Scottish demons and spirits, the simple dictionary definition of ghosts is inadequate, so many are the different types of ghost in the country's spectral-lore. Folklorists have devised this classification series for Scottish ghosts:

A *ghost* is a stranger to the one who perceives it.
An *apparition* is well-known to the percipient, and can be a parent, relative, or friend.
A *vision* is the appearance of a religious figure.
A *poltergeist* is a projection of an energy that finds its potential through the frustrated creativity of adolescence, and emanates from the living rather than from the dead.

These basic categories are sub-divided again into a further six classifications:

Harbingers of death: These appear with pale minatory fingers and sightless eyes and beckon the percipient to doom, or bring their gloomy presage of death to others.
Load or resident ghosts.
Phantasms of the living: People appearing in spirit form when they are known to be elsewhere.
Telepathic apparitions: Seen by more than one person.
Ghosts that were neper human, like animals and objects.
Ghostly music, lights and allied phenomena.

Of all the categories, we have three which appear in almost

every part of Scotland in folklore relics. Ghostly dogs leading to family treasure or safety, ghosts being earthbound because they have things yet to do, and people cured of gambling by wagering with ghosts.

Disbelief in spectres of the dead is a comparatively recent attitude of mind, for as late as the seventeenth century ghosts still had a respectable standing in Scotland. This was to tip over into the literary styles of the eighteenth and nineteenth centuries. Every writer of note in Scotland once believed that to be successfully rounded in a literary sense they had to include the ghost story in their collections of writings. Writers like James Hogg (1770–1835) and Walter Scott (1771–1832) believed that ghosts were a part of the very fabric of Scots culture.

Yet another skein in that fabric was Scotland's involvement in witch-lore.

Witchcraft in Scottish Folklore

Between the Protestant Reformation (1559) and the Union of the Parliaments (1707) in excess of three thousand people died dreadfully in Scotland because their perverted accusers believed/pretended they were witches. Witchcraft as it appears in Scottish folklore then, is a late sixteenth-century phenomenon. Scotland's developed beliefs in witchcraft marched alongside race memories of nature worship and fairylore to give it some substance of, albeit false, reality. This was eventually developed by Scotland's witch-hunters to prove that witchcraft skills could be inherited and that witchcraft had a history of its own. In pre-Reformation Scotland the medieval church had been more interested in hunting down heresy against Holy Mother Church than in the supposed magic conjurings of witchcraft. Medieval clergy, too, believed that some witches did good things through herbal medicine, for instance, while other set evil curses and the like, but all believed that the best policy against witches was to leave them alone lest you stir up supernatural forces.

That was until witchcraft was made a culpable heresy in Europe. Along with the European influences of political, religious and economic thought in the sixteenth century, there also came to Scotland a belief in the reality and seriousness of witchcraft and that wherever it occurred it had to be rooted out.

The Geneva-based French Protestant reformer and theologian John Calvin said all witches 'shall be put to death'. This theme influenced the Scottish reformer John Knox, who cleverly juxtaposed 'the Devil, the Mass and Witches' for his own partisan denominational ends. Both expounded the authority of Exodus 22:18: 'Thou shalt not suffer a witch to live'. Thus the Presbyterians (and Episcopalians too, in the seventeenth century) set about rooting out witchcraft with a will. It must be said, though, that north of Perthshire and in the Hebrides witch persecution was hardly known, as the old ways of nature worship were never linked with heresy, political expediency or social unrest.

It was the Victorian writers who attempted to give witchcraft a long history in Scotland, quoting such sixteenth-century sources as George Buchanan's *History of Scotland* who averred that King Duffus (962–66) was attacked by witches. The likes of the Victorian Presbyterian cleric the Rev. Walter Gregor, writing in 1881, provided a stock definition of the perceived witch of Scottish superstition and folklore. He wrote:

The witch was usually an old woman, who lives in a lonely house by herself, and kept all her affairs very much to herself. Her power was derived from Satan, and was very great, and ranged over almost everything. By various ways she could cause disease in man and beast; raise storms to destroy crops, sink ships, and do other destructive work; steal cows' milk, and keep herself well supplied with milk and butter, though she had no cow. To do this last she was able to turn herself into a hare. At times, however, she used her power for the benefit of those who pleased her.

In 1736 the 1604 Act Anentis Witchcraft was repealed and Scotland's law regarding witchcraft was brought into line with

England's. Some Presbyterian extremists considered this to be an abomination and said that the repeal was 'contrary to the express law of God'.

Memories of the locations of witch executions and where witches were supposed to dwell live on in Scottish place-names. Here are a few:

The Witch's Gravestone (*Leac na Bana-bhuidseach*)
  – South Uist.
Witches' Cairn – Yester, Lothian; and Foulden,
  Berwickshire.
Witches' Stone – Ratho and Spott, Lothian.
Witches' Wa' – Closeburn, Dumfries & Galloway.

The Scots Devil

The fact that the Devil was alive and well in Scotland was never doubted from medieval times and he appears in the country's literature, history and folklore. A true picture of Scotland's Devil becomes clear when the witch inquisitors began their work in the sixteenth century. He was not the Horned God of Celtic legend, but the Christian Satan of Isaiah – 'How art thou fallen from heaven, O Lucifer, son of the morning'.

Although Scotland developed its own Devil in book and ballad, his appearance is not uniform. In Border folklore, for instance, he can appear in various disguises from black ram to brindled cat. In no other country in Europe did the Devil take on so many tradesman's guises; we see him as black-smith, cobbler, carpenter and musician. The poet Robert Burns (1759–96) cocked a snook at received Presbyterian belief that music and dance were the Devil's work with his couplet from 'The Deil's awa wi' the' Exciseman':

The Deil cam' fiddlin' through the town,
And danc'd awa wi' th' Exciseman.

Scottish folklore and proverbs are fecund with Devil super-stition and in no other nation's language has the Devil so many nicknames from Auld Clootie and The Earl o' Hell, to Auld Waghorn and Auld Sandie. And here are some locations which the Devil made his own in Scotland:

Deil's Stanes – Urquhart, Morayshire.
Deil's Cradle – Balgarthno, Angus.
Deil's Dyke – New Cumnock, Ayrshire; also at
    Mingaff and Inch, Dumfries & Galloway.
Deil's Mitten – Longformacus, Berwickshire.
Devil's Staircase – Glencoe, Argyllshire.
Devil's Cauldron – Lednock River, Perthshire.
Devil's Elbow – Braemar, Aberdeenshire.
Devil's Beef Tub – Moffat, Dumfries & Galloway.
Hell's Lum [*Chimney*] – Pennan, Aberdeenshire.

Thoughts on Modern Scottish Folklore

Folklore has always been found in urban as well as rural situations. Indeed folklore can be discovered anywhere that society has developed. Even in modern times folklore remains what ordinary people believe and what they do because of these beliefs. Much of our daily behaviour is regulated by our belief in our churches' teachings, our political prejudices, how we perceive morality, as well as apprehended knowledge of law, science and the arts, but a good deal is regulated by what we were taught by, or picked up from, our parents and grandparents or any other members of previous generations. Moreover, new customs and new beliefs, new superstitions, are coming into existence very day. Some of these will survive to become folklore and the foundations of the folk belief of tomorrow.

Thus the folklore of commerce and industry is a strong strain too in Scottish folklore. Blacksmiths, for instance, who were traditionally the first of tradesmen because they made the implement of others, have a rich folklore. So too have miners and seamen. There's industrial folklore in apprenticeship completion rituals, topping-out ceremonies for new buildings and the laying of foundation stones. All of them are based on the acts carried out to petition and placate the old gods of Scotland's primitive tribes, and in time the very technology we use every day from lasers to computers will become part of the fabric of the folklore of our modern age.

Gazetteer

A

Abbotsford, Melrose, Borders   GHOST

In 1811 Sir Walter Scott (1771–1832) purchased, for 4,000 guineas, the little farmhouse and steading of Clartyhole from the parish minister of Galashiels, the Rev. Dr Robert Douglas. Scott changed the name to Abbotsford – as the land had once been owned by the monks of Melrose Abbey who had used the nearby ford across the Tweed – and in 1822 the old farmhouse was pulled down to build the present mansion.

Scott's friend, the London cabinet-maker and antiques dealer George Bulloch, gave him some useful advice on the earlier renovations to Abbotsford, and it was the supposed presage of Bulloch's death that gave the house one of its curious ghost stories, which Scott himself recorded.

On 30 April 1818, Scott wrote to his friend, the actor Daniel Terry, that his in the process of being renovated home was exposed to a 'mysterious disturbance'. He wrote:

The night before last we were awakened by a violent noise, like drawing heavy boards along the new part of the house. I fancied something had fallen, and thought no more about it. This was about two in the morning. Last night, at the same witching hour, the very same noise occurred. Mrs. S[cott], as you know, is rather timbersome, *so up I got, with Beardie's [his great-grandfather Walter Scott] broadsword under my arm … But nothing was out of order, neither can I discover what occasioned the disturbance.*

Scott went on that

> *the noise resembled half a dozen men hard at work putting up boards and furniture, and nothing can be more certain than that there was nobody on the premises at the time.*

A few days after the letter's dispatch, Scott was shocked to hear of Bulloch's death from Terry and that the cabinet-maker had died at the very hour that Scott and his family had experienced the disturbances. Thereafter, whenever a story of ghostly personal experience was called for at a folklore gathering, Scott would tell of George Bulloch's psychic presence.

Aberdeen, Grampian   WITCHES

In all there were some fifty witchcraft trials of note reported in the City of Aberdeen during 1536–1669, and several other cases within the county.

The most famous was the case of Old Janet Wishart who was a victim of the witch craze which engulfed Aberdeen and was later intensified as a result of the publication in 1597 of King James VI's pernicious book *Daemonologie*. In the early part of his reign the king firmly believed in witchcraft – and that such as the North Berwick Witches were working magic against him – and he personally supervised the torture of some of them to extract confessions.

Old Janet Wishart, Mrs John Leyis, was accused and indicted of casting a *cantrip* (the old Scots word for magic spell) on one Alexander Thompson. The result was that Thompson shivered with the ague alternatively with rolling in his own sweat. Likewise she was said to have enchanted Andrew Webster to death. Many a neighbour, too, testified that she had cast the Evil Eye over them, had set malevolent cats to assail them, raised storms and fires and caused dreadful nightmares about dismembered corpses. Her trial and execution was held at Aberdeen on 23 February 1596 and she was strangled and burned at the stake at a cost of £3 13s 4d (£3.66½p).

The modern village of Aberfoyle, east of Loch Ard, is known as the 'Gateway to the Trossachs'. Its churchyard still sports the mortsafes reminding of the gruesome early nineteenth-century exploits of the grave-robbers whose leading lights were the body-snatchers William Burke and William Hare who were brought to justice at Edinburgh in 1828. A mile or so east of Aberfoyle was the now vanished Clachan of Aberfoyle, where Frank Osbaldistone and Bailie Nicol Jarvie ventured in Sir Walter Scott's *Rob Roy* (1818) to meet the famous folk hero. Here too, hanging from a tree opposite the eponymous hotel is the plough coulter ('Bailie Nicol Jarvie's Poker') which Scott mentions in reference to the bailie.

Since the 1994 internationally acclaimed film about his exploits, Rob Roy Macgregor has expanded in stature as a folk hero. In simple summary Rob Roy (1671–1734) was a Scottish freebooter, the second son of Lt. Col. Donald Macgregor of Glengyle. Rob lived at first as a grazier at Balquhidder fending off the northern outlaws who came to steal his cattle; at length he set up a band of followers to protect himself and his neighbours who paid 'protection money' for his services. He espoused the Jacobite cause and, on purchasing the lands of Craigroyston and Inversnaid, laid claim to the chieftainship of the Clan Gregor, a clan long proscribed in name and property. Falling into debt, Rob Roy's lands were seized and he declared open revolt on his creditor the Duke of Montrose. Today a whole folklore has built around his exploits, based on the exaggerations of Scott's novel.

As a folk hero Scott personified Rob Roy Macgregor as the denizen of the Highland warrior's way of life which was being pushed aside by the so-called civilising influence of the Lowland administrators, of whom Bailie Nicol Jarvie was the representative. By 1720 Rob Roy had settled peacefully at Balquhidder, where he died at the age of sixty-three. He was buried in the churchyard on the knoll above Loch Voil.

A contemporary of Rob Roy was the Rev. Robert Kirk. He was the author of *The Secret Commonwealth of Elves, Fauns and Fairies*. As a penance for revealing the little folks' secrets, it is said that when he died in 1692 his soul was claimed by them and incarcerated in nearby Aberfoyle Fairy Hill.

Abergeldie, Grampian   GHOST

On the south bank of the River Dee stands the turreted square tower of Abergeldie Castle, which was royally leased from 1848 and became the Highland home of King Edward VII when he was Prince of Wales. Some three miles north of Abergeldie, at the confluence of the Fearder Burn and the Dee, once stood the Old Mill of Inver, long haunted, it was said by the wraith known as The Black Hand.

For many decades the mill was run by the Davidsons. In 1767 one John Davidson claimed that he saw the renowned spectre while going about his business at the mill. It was one of Scotland's rarer phantoms in that it materialised as a black, ganglinous, human hand severed at the wrist. Davidson was not surprised to see the hand for its reputation of terrorising the neighbourhood at its own whim was well known. It seems that Davidson challenged the spectral owner of the hand to reveal why the appendage appeared. Local lore recounts that the spectre wished to be reunited with the sword which it had grasped before being severed in combat.

Long after, Davidson pointed out a basket-hilted sword above his fireplace. The weapon, he said, was the one lost and that he had dug it up in the mill yard where the hand had directed.

The severed hand of a person hanged at the public gallows was long considered efficacious in Scottish magic lore; such a hand was pickled then used as a candle holder at ceremonies wherein it was called a 'Hand of Glory'.

Abernyte, Tayside   WITCHLORE

Many a Scottish parish owned a ducking-stool, or ducking-halter for the testing of witches. The concept was that if a person was innocent of witchcraft then they would sink; if guilty they would float by magic means. The hamlet of Abernyte had such a custom and for many decades a pool was pointed out as the one where witches had been so tested.

Allanton, Berwickshire, Borders

The old house at Allanbank, once reached from the north gate of the also-demolished Blackadder House, Allanton, was razed to the ground in the 1800s, yet, it was to be the scene of one of the best-loved of all the romantic Border folktales. The story was first given a wider audience by the antiquary Charles Kirkpatrick Sharp (1781–1851) of Hoddom Castle, Annandale, when he collected an outline of the story from his old nurse Jenny Blackadder, who had been a servant at Allanbank.

'Pearlin' Jean – the Border name for the type of lace, pearling, she wore – was the wraith of a French woman which Jenny Blackadder 'often heard ... rustling in silks up and down the stairs, and along the passages'. While Jenny was courting her yet-to-be husband Thomas Blackadder they

> made an assignation to meet one moonlight night in the orchard at Allanbank. True Thomas, of course, was the first comer and seeing a female figure in a light-coloured dress at some distance, he ran forward with open arms to embrace his Jenny, when lo, and behold! as he neared the spot where the figure stood it vanished, and presently he saw it again at the very end of the orchard, a considerable way off. Thomas went home in a fright, but Jenny, who came last, and saw nothing, forgave him, and they were married.

It is recorded, too, that the housekeeper Betty Norrie had seen 'Pearlin' Jean often at Allanbank. But how did her story begin?

It evolved in the Paris of King Louis XIV and the main players were Jeanne, who was to become immortal as 'Pearlin' Jean, and Robert Stuart, before he inherited his family baronetcy in 1687. They had been lovers and Jeanne overhead Stuart tell his drinking cronies that he was leaving France and

Jeanne behind. They were to have an emotive parting; Jeanne was tearful and Stuart was rough in telling her he was finished with her. She berated him for going home to marry a Scots woman, and he flung money on the table for her as though she were a common whore.

Stuart stormed out of his Paris lodgings to his waiting carriage and climbed aboard, wrenching his coat-tails from Jeanne's persistent grasp. He slammed the carriage door and ordered his postillion to drive away.

As the vehicle sprang into life, Jeanne, who had been screaming at him through the carriage window, 'You cannot ever escape my love,' fell from the step and was run over by the back wheels. She was killed instantly, but Stuart ordered his coach not to stop.

At length Stuart returned to Scotland with his new bride Jean, daughter of Sir John Gilmour. They were making their way back to Allanbank for the first time since their marriage, and as their coach turned into the drive at Allanbank the vehicle shuddered to a halt. Stuart stuck his head out of the carriage window and asked the postillion why they had stopped. The ashen-faced servant pointed ahead towards the gateway. There on the keystone of the arch knelt the spectre of Jeanne, her face smeared with blood. Stuart remembered Jeanne's last screamed words to him, 'I shall be in Scotland before you.' As Stuart and his new wife watched appalled, the wraith of Jeanne slowly dematerialised.

Jeanne's ghost now took up permanent residence appearing 'in rustling silks and the patter of high-heeled shoes'. Her appearance was attested by many Allanbank visitors and servants from the nearby villages of Allanton, Edrom and Chirnside. Stuart even tried to placate the ghost by having her portrait hung next to that of his wife. He even invited a pulpit of ministers to allay her troubled spirit. But Jeanne was having nothing of clerics of the Reformed Faith and she continued to haunt.

Stuart married Helen Cockburn as his second wife and still Jeanne kept them company. At last Stuart died and for a hundred years Jeanne remained in the house, but those who saw her reported that she changed from being a spectral beauty in a bloodstained gown to a skeleton in a winding sheet. When the old house was demolished locals speculated whether Jeanne would go too. Indeed she was never seen again. A great new mansion house and dower house were built for the Blackadder estate where Allanbank had stood. They have gone too, but the old folk still remember the jingle associated with the story of 'Pearlin' Jean:

For all the silver in English bank,
Nor yet for all the gold.
Would I pass through the hall of Allanbank,
When the midnight bell was told.

Alloway, Ayrshire   FOLK HERO

The Robert Burns Birthplace Museum at Alloway encapsulates all the lore about the poet that any enthusiast would wish, but because Burns is feted as a competent and couthy literary and national Scottish hero around the world on his birthdate of 25 January, his contribution to the preserving of elements of Scottish folklore is somewhat forgotten.

In many of his poems, like 'Hallowe'en' and 'Address to the Deil', Burns mentions Scottish folklore memories that were being forgotten even in his day, and thereby he preserved them. As a child Robert Burns had listened to an 'old Maid of my Mother's', he wrote in his autobiographical letter to Dr John Moore, called Elizabeth Davidson who had the 'largest [*oral*] collection in the country of tales and songs concerning devils, ghosts, fairies, brownies, witches, warlocks, spunkies, kelpies, elf-candles, dead-lights, wraiths, apparitions, cantraips, enchanted towers, giants, dragons, and other trumpery'. To this fount of folklore memory Burns paid tribute and averred that it 'cultivated the latent seeds of poesy; but had so strong an effect on my imagination, that to this hour, in my nocturnal rambles I sometimes keep a sharp lookout in suspicious places; and though nobody can be more sceptical in these matters than I, yet it often takes an effort of Philosophy to shake off these idle terrors'.

Alves, Morayshire

On the summit of the Knock of Alves, in the Laigh of Moray, stands York Tower, commemorating HRH Prince Frederick, Duke of York (1763–1803), son of George III. The lore of the place has nothing to do with Hanoverian myth, but to older and darker roots. It has long been a place associated with the fairies who gather on windy nights to screetch and chatter. It is still pointed out, too, as the place where Macbeth met Shakespeare's three 'Weird Sisters'.

Ancrum, Roxburghshire, Borders

The village of Ancrum is situated on a bend in the River Ale. A viewpoint in the area is Peniel Heugh Hill, sporting its Waterloo Monument set up in 1815 by the Marquis of Lothian and his tenants to mark the end of the Napoleonic conflict. These are the hills and the forests in which the locals hid when the next swathe of violence overwhelmed them in antiquity. Being on the border between Scotland and England the local folk suffered many a raid. Here in 1544 the Earl of Hertford burned the village on his way back to England. The Scots, though, had their revenge the next year when an English force led by Sir Brian Latoun and Sir Ralph Evers were challenged and routed on Ancrum Moor by the Earl of Angus and Scott of Buccleuch.

On the high ground of the battle at Lillyat (now called Lilliard's Edge) there is a marker to tell of the courage of the folk heroine Lilliard, the Maid of Teviotdale. When she saw her lover killed in the conflict, she seized a sword and fought to the death. Her stone reads:

> *Fair maiden Lilliard lies under this stane;*
> *Little was her stature, but great was her fame;*
> *Upon the English loons she laid mony thumps,*
> *And when her legs were cuttid off, she fought on her*
> *stumps.*

The ancient red-sandstone royal burgh of Annan – named for the river on which it stands – was a stronghold of the Bruces and the home of Robert de Brus 'The Competitor', Lord of Annandale, grandfather of Robert I, The Bruce. Ever since the twelfth century the Bruces considered themselves cursed. Robert Bruce believed his contracting leprosy was 'the finger of God upon me' and a consequence of the family's execration. Folklore says the bad luck came about in this way.

During his visit to the then castle hamlet of Annan in 1138, the Irish Bishop of Armagh, Maolmhaodhog ua Morgair, named St Malachy O'More, was entertained at the Bruce's castle (the last traces of which were removed in 1875). While he ate, Malachy overheard servants speaking about a robber who was to be hanged. Malachy asked his host – the chief lawman of the district – to spare the robber, and Brus agreed to do so.

Malachy left soon after his repast and as he rode out of the town he saw the cadaver of the robber hanging by the roadside. Angered that Brus had lied to him, Malachy laid a curse on Brus, his family, and the little castle hamlet. After Malachy died in 1148, Robert de Brus paid for lights to be maintained at the shrine of St Malachy at the monastery of Clairvaux, France, where the soon-to-be saint had died. But folklore has it that Malachy's curse was never expiated.

Another story was also associated with 'St Malachy's Curse on Annan'. Celtic myth speaks of blood-drinking spirits, even though the romanticism of the vampire is largely an eighteenth-century invention, and Scottish folklore does not dwell much on the vampire of folklore even though some devotees point to Cruden Bay, Aberdeenshire, as the supposed birthplace of the inspiration that gave the Irish writer Bram Stoker (1847–1912) his Count Dracula.

It seems that not long after the laying of Malachy's curse the plague came to Annan, spread by a man on the run from Yorkshire. The Bruces had given the man sanctuary, but Annan soon regretted the family's generosity as the man continued the 'wickedness' that had led him to flee, and the man succumbed to the plague.

Not long after he had been buried, locals reported seeing the man around Annan accompanied by 'a horrible crowd of dogs'. Terrified by the sight of the ambulant 'rotting corpse', the good folk of Annan sent for priests to come and cleanse the place with their prayers. Alas the plague raged, all spread, said the locals, by the undead visitation.

One evening the Bruces were holding a banquet for the clergy visiting the burgh to drive out the plague with new prayers they had composed, when two brothers started a conversation concerning the death of their father in the plague. The upshot was that they volunteered to rid Annan of the dread monster and wreak their own revenge for their father's death.

As the banquet went on the two young men slipped out of the castle and through the silent streets of Annan to where the plague man had been buried. They resolved to disinter the cadaver and destroy it by fire, so they both set about digging.

At last they came to the body and observed that it had 'swollen with much enormous corpulence, and the face red and swollen above measure'. Yet the clothes in which the man had been buried seemed to have been cut as if the body had been trying to escape from its mortal trappings.

One of the two men could not contain his anger any longer as he remembered the fate of his father and, taking up the sharp spade with which he had dug the grave, he brought its point down upon the chest of the corpse with great force. He let free a huge issue of blood which soaked their feet as they stood in the shallow grave. It was more blood than any human body might have contained and the two young men realised that they had disinterred a vampire still full of its victims' blood.

The cadaver was hauled out of the grave and dragged through the streets to the edge of town, where the two young men placed it on a pyre. Remembering the old superstition that the vampire could not be destroyed without removing the heart, this was done by a few deft strokes of the spade.

As they tossed the heart separately into the flames the cadaver let out a huge sigh and was consumed. Thereafter Annan was never affected by the plague again.

Applecross, Ross & Cromarty   STONES

The fishing village of Applecross, with its eponymous bay on the Inner Sound of Raasay, has an emotive stone circle with a central holed stone. For centuries it was a meeting place for communal worship and ritual of a pagan nature. So efficacious were its stones considered for the cure of disease and foretelling the future, that in 1656 the Presbytery of Dingwall condemned the locals for resorting to the holed stone. The practice was for the petitioner to put his or her head through the stone to obtain an omen for the success of a journey or enterprise.

Ardbeg, Islay, Inner Hebrides   NORSE/FAIRYLORE

The old records have it that the Gaelic name for the isle of Islay, *Ile*, is derived from that of the Danish Princess Ila, who walked to this, the most southerly of the Hebridean islands from Ireland. She had accomplished this by stepping from stone to stone, all of which mysteriously appeared in the sea to make her journey possible. The old folk pointed out her grave – a standing stone above Knock Bay – and counselled all never to try to open this grave for it was enchanted; those who tried would be rendered insane.

The Hill of Ile was deemed to be a northern home of the Queen of Elfhame. From here she dispenses wisdom to all women who imbibed from a fairy cup which the queen kept within the hill. Those who were dull-witted were said in the locality to be 'Still sitting on the Hill of Ile when the wisdom cup was emptied'.

Ardrossan, Ayrshire   FOLK HERO/SORCERY

Famous as a port and bathing place, Ardrossan was long an important departure quay for Arran, Northern Ireland and the Isle of Man. Its folkloric relevance stems from its relic twelfth-century castle, for centuries an important base of the Anglo-Norman Lowland clan of the Montgomerys. The castle is associated with the folk hero Sir William Wallace (*c.* 1274–1305), the premier champion of Scottish independence who won a decisive victory over the English at Stirling Bridge in 1297. In Ardrossan Castle was to be found a certain dungeon known as 'Wallace's Larder' where he imprisoned the English soldiers he captured. It is not surprising to find that the castle is deemed to be haunted by Wallace. Before Wallace's time, folklore records show, the castle was the home of a certain sorcerer known as the 'Deil o' Ardrossan', who was buried in the local churchyard. Soil from the sorcerer's grave, said the superstitious, would raise a tempest if thrown into the sea.

Athelstaneford, East Lothian   SALTIRE/PATRON SAINT

Next to St Andrews, Athelstaneford, at the foot of the Garleton Hills by the Cogtail Burn, is the most famous site of the cult of the Apostle and Martyr St Andrew of Bethsaida in Galilee. A number of medieval stories tell how St Andrew's relics came to Scotland, but certainly his cult was established at St Andrews (then known as *Cennrigmonaid*), 'the headland of the king's mount' by the eighth century, and from the influence of his shrine at St Andrews Cathedral the Apostle became Scotland's patron saint.

St Andrew's association with Athelstaneford may be attributed to such historians as Andrew of Wyntoun and Walter Bower. They recounted how an army of the Picts led by Hungus (Angus) was encamped in a land called the *Merc*, which they interpreted as the Merse, the territory between the Lammermuir Hills and the River Tweed. At this time the area as far as the Forth was Northumbrian territory and a force of the Angles under Athelstane was moving north. Knowing that a battle was inevitable Hungus was walking with his *comitibus* (earls) discussing strategy, when he saw in the sky a blinding light and heard a voice telling him to advance against the enemy, bearing the cross of his army's patron St Andrew. To underline the advice a huge cloud formation formed a white saltire (the *crux decusata*, the diagonal cross on which St Andrew is said to have been martyred). Hungus did as advised and the Picts won a great battle at what is now Athelstaneford, and the saltire was eventually adopted as Scotland's national flag. Today the folkloric legend of the saltire and St Andrew are marked in the village churchyard with a memorial.

Auchencrow, Berwickshire, Borders WITCHCRAFT

Called Edencraw by the locals, this village once had an abnormally large number of elderberry bushes in its vicinity. These were to keep at bay the witches for which the hamlet was famed. Up on Horsely Hill the witches were tried and the last of the accused, Margaret Girvin, died as late as 1806. Records show that in 1700 Thomas Cook of nearby Chirnside was indicted for attacking a supposed witch who he believed was assailing his family.

Auchterderran, Fife DUELLING

Scottish folklore's richest stories about duelling concern giants hurling great boulders at each other across the countryside to form mountain ranges, hazards in river-beds and extraneous rocks in fields.

Duelling was an important part of medieval law and chivalry. There are three types of duel reflected in folktales. First there was the judicial duel, which was a variation of the earlier form of so-called 'Judgement by God'. It manifested, too, in the 'ordeal' by fire and water, often mentioned in Scotland's witch trials. Then there was the duel of chivalry, carried out usually as a fight between knights. Thirdly, was the duel of honour, when a person's own or country's honour was at stake.

Someone, folktale tells us, actually fought for the honour of Scotland. In 1390 John, Lord Welles, the English ambassador to Scotland made discouraging remarks about the courage of the Scots and he challenged any Scottish knight to fight it out. His challenge was taken up by Sir David de

Lindsay. They duelled on Old London Bridge on 6 May 1390 in the presence of Richard II and his queen. At length the Scottish knight unseated Lord Welles and instead of finishing him off with a dagger – as the crowd anticipated – Lindsay spared his adversary and Scottish courage and honour were saved.

Folklore would have it that the escapades of the youngest of Scotland's duellers, and the last duel to take place in Scotland, were enacted in Fife.

There is the story that the Rev. Dr Alexander Bell (1753–1832), founder of The Madras College at St Andrews, took part in a duel at the age of sixteen. He seems to have had a quarrel with a boy called Crookenden and they decided to duel it out. The two boys met at Witch Hill, overlooking St Andrews Bay by the road now known as The Scores, and decided to use muskets. Bell was so short-sighted that he fired at his seconds instead of his adversary, and as both boys missed they decided upon a thankful reconciliation. After 1726, of course, duelling had technically become an attempted murder charge, but the local authorities seem to have turned a blind eye.

The last recorded duel in Scotland took place on 2 August 1826 in a field at Cardenbarns, Auchterderran, north-east of Kirkcaldy. The duel took place between David Landale, a Kirkcaldy bleacher and merchant, and George Morgan, agent for the Bank of Scotland. Apparently Morgan had slandered Landale, and Landale hit Morgan over the head with his umbrella. As no apology was extracted from either party they decided to duel out their differences with pistols. At the tryst Morgan fired first, but before time; he missed. Landale fired and did not miss. The merchant was arrested and was sent for trial at Perth where the jury acquitted him. Landale lived on in Kirkcaldy for many years after that and was a respected citizen.

Auchtermuchty, Fife   DEVIL

The village of Auchtermuchty, from the Gaelic for 'height of the swineherds', was once known for its thatched roofs (in contrast with the more common pantiles of Fife). It enters folklore records, though, because of its supposed attack by the Devil. In centuries past the folk of Auchtermuchty were recognised for their piety, a quality, the old story relates, which irritated the Devil himself. In order to tempt the villagers into more wanton ways of life, the Devil appeared amongst them one day dressed as a Presbyterian minister. As the village had no church of its own at that time, the Devil preached in the square and so inspired all who heard him that he quickly built up a following.

One day as the Devil preached, a man called Robin Ruthven caught sight of the Devil's feet beneath his cloak. Instead of shoes Ruthven clearly saw cloven hooves. In a moment Ruthven denounced the Devil who rose above the rooftops 'like a fiery dragon' in his anger, and this is why, said the Border poet, James Hogg (1770–1835), it is not easy to get an Auchtermuchty person to heed a sermon, for they think 'aye that [they see] the cloven foot peeping out from beneath every sentence'.

Auldearn, Nairn, Grampian   WITCHES

The wooded area called Hardmuir was once a heathland and was one of the locations pointed out as the place where Macbeth and Banquo met the witches.

Auldearn was to be the scene of four witch trials between April and September 1662, of which the most celebrated was that of Isobel Goudie. Sir Hew Campbell of Calder was granted a commission to bring her to trial, the proceedings of which gave the whole resume of the popular superstitions of the day concerning witchcraft. Goudie confessed to having a pact with the Devil and supported the popular belief that witches met in a coven of thirteen persons; her particular witching skill was galeanthropy (being able to turn herself into a cat). From her trial records came the infamous grace which witches were supposed to intone before their feasting:

We eat this meat in the Devil's name,
With much sorrow and muckle shame;   much

We shall destroy both house and hold;
Both sheep and cattle in the fold,
Little good shall come to the fore,
Of all the rest of the little store.

The prehistoric stone circle at Auldearn was cited as the place where Isobel Goudie met the Devil and his cohorts of demons, and the old kirk was where she was said to have undergone her witch initiation.

B

Badenoch, Inverness   NORSE/VEGETATION

The wild hills and glens of Badenoch – bounded by Lochaber, Braemar, the peaks of the Central Grampians and the summits of the Monadhliath Mountains – were owned in antiquity by the Comyns and then by the royal Stewarts. In the folklore of these clans is the story of how the great Caledonian Forest around Badenoch was destroyed by a Scandinavian king in a fit of jealousy. The king sent a fiery winged beast called a *Muime* to fling blazing brands through-out the forest to destroy it by incineration. Before all the forest could be destroyed the *muime* was killed by a Badenoch hunter using a silver bullet.

Ballantrae, Ayrshire   CURSE/CANNIBALISM/GHOST

Even though Robert Louis Stevenson did visit the coastal village of Ballantrae in 1876 – and claimed that the populace stoned him out of the place for the eccentricity of his dress – he did not set his book *The Master of Ballantrae* (1889) in the neighbourhood. At the date of his visit, however, a popular ghost story was doing the rounds. The tale concerned the ghost of Sawney Bean, a celebrated seventeenth-century murderer who ate his victims. Bean was thus famous in the history of Scottish folklore as instances of cannibalism are rare north of the Tweed–Solway line.

Bean's ghost is said to haunt the family's cave beneath

Bennane Head, north of Ballantrae. Here the Beans had taken up residence when Bean's common-law wife, Black Agnes Douglas, had been driven out of Ballantrae as a witch. For twenty-five years, folklore says, they and their family lived in the cave and survived by eating the cadavers of waylaid travellers.

At last King James VI & I sent a posse of men with bloodhounds to flush them out, and in the cave the posse discovered human limbs hanging from the roof and an assortment of mortal flesh pickled in barrels. Bean, Agnes and their forty-six assorted family members were rounded up and taken to Edinburgh for execution. Before he died, Bean put a curse on the cave and thereafter strange incidents have been recorded nearby. Even up to modern times the police have logged reports from drivers along the nearby roads having to break sharply to avoid ghostly figures.

Banff, Grampian   FOLK HERO

Unlike King Arthur, Robin Hood is not mentioned much in Scotland, though in 1420 the historian Andrew of Wyntoun mentions him in his *Chronicle*:

> *Then Little John and Robin Hood*
> *As forest outlaws were well renowned*
> *All this time they plied their trade.*

In 1555 the Scottish parliament forbade the impersonation of Robin Hood and Little John in open-air plays in royal burghs on pain of five years' imprisonment; they feared that Robin's outlawry would give others romantic ideas of rebellion. Nevertheless various places did dub people 'The Robin Hood of …'. One such was James MacPherson.

The bastard son of a gypsy and a local laird, James MacPherson was hanged for his outlawry at Banff in 1700. He had taken up with his mother's people and had pursued a life robbing the rich farmers of Banffshire and giving their goods and money to the poor. In particular he fell foul of Laird Duff of Braco who mounted a posse to track him down.

MacPherson was surrounded and taken at a fair when a woman threw a blanket over him from an upstairs window as he was making an escape. Condemned to death, MacPherson is said to have sat at the gallow's foot and played a tune he had just composed; 'MacPherson's Rant' is still on the programme at fiddlers' rallies. On finishing his tune he stood up and offered his fiddle to any MacPherson who might be present in the crowd gathered to witness the execution. None came forward so MacPherson broke the instrument over his executioner's head and launched himself into immortality from the gallows. His broken fiddle is still displayed at the Clan MacPherson House Museum, Newtonmore.

Ben Macdhui, Aberdeenshire   MONSTER

At 4,296 feet, Ben Macdhui is the highest peak in the Cairngorms, and is the setting for one of the most persistent of all Scottish tales about monsters.The terrifying creature is known as the Grey Man of Macdhui and stands ten feet tall to taunt and bring doom to the climbers and ramblers who meet him.

Attested reports about the monster began in Victorian times and one such came from Professor Norman Collie (1859–1942) of the Department of Organic Chemistry in the University of London. A no-nonsense scientist and a keen mountaineer, Collie said that while he was walking on Ben Macdhui in 1891 he became aware of the sound of feet following him, but the reverberating steps seemed two or three times the span of a normal gait. He stopped, listened, and peered into the mist but saw nothing. The professor felt a panic state overtaking him and he fled towards Rothiemurchus Forest.

Such footfalls have been attested by many along with a feeling of sinister presence. An actual figure of enormous size was seen emerging from the Lairig Ghru by mountaineer A.M. Kellas in the years after World War I. Others, including Honorary Sheriff-substitute George Duncan in 1914, have recorded the figure as wearing a robe and a 'lum [top] hat'.

Berneray, Harris, Outer Hebrides

The old folktale says that should you observe three duns aligned in a certain way at Dunan Hill Fort you will have found the spot where treasure lies. Once he or she has the three duns so in view, they must then throw a hat or coat onto the ground and the treasure will reveal itself. The story was first written down from oral sources by folklorists in the 1890s who averred that the site had been a ritual place of the *Druides* in antiquity. The throwing of a garment here was deemed a folk relic of sacrifice or libation to the spirits of the place.

Birnam, Tayside

The narrow Pass of Birnam, between Birnam Hill and the River Tay, was known as the 'Mouth of the Highlands' and traversed by armies, drovers and travellers, including many who have added to Scotland's story. In terms of folklore, Birnam is a key location for legends about Macbeth.

Despite his bad image depicted in Shakespeare's play, Macbeth ruled well and generously. He was born in 1005 son of Findlaech, Mormaer (High Steward) of Moray, and one of the daughters of Malcolm II. In the summer of 1040 Macbeth was crowned High King of Scotland at Scone, and was slain at Lumphanan in 1057. There is no contemporary evidence that Macbeth was a murderer (King Duncan, for instance, was killed at the Battle of Burghead and not by Macbeth's hand) and modern historians can totally discredit Shakespeare's picture of him. Folklore locations at Birnam associated with Macbeth are 'Birnam Oaks', the survivors of Shakespeare's 'Great Birnam Wood' on the south bank of the Tay, and Duncan's Castle (a hill-fort on Birnam Hill) and Dunsinane, one of the summits of the Sidlaws.

Blackness, West Lothian

The seventeenth-century House of the Binns near Blackness was built by the Edinburgh merchant Thomas Dalyell, and was inherited by his son General Tom 'Bloody Tam' Dalyell (*c.*1599–1685).

Following a career of military exploits Tam Dalyell joined the Royalist expedition that ended with the Battle of Worcester in 1651 and King Charles II's flight to France. Escaping from the Tower of London, Dalyell saw foreign service in Russia fighting for the Czar, but, at the Restoration of the Stuarts, Charles II gave him command of the army in Scotland. Thus Dalyell raised the Royal Scots Greys in 1681.

Because of his rumbustuous and eccentric character, Dalyell was forged into a larger-than-life character in folklore and was credited by his enemies in the Covenanters as an associate of the Devil. The myths about Dalyell's satanic friendship was given a high profile in Sir Walter Scott's book *Redgauntlet* (1824) for in the tale told by Wandering Willie, Dalyell is glimpsed in Hell with the Devil. It is even reported that when General Tam built a new range onto The Binns the Devil threatened to blow down the walls. To this threat the General countered: 'I will build me a turret at every corner to pin down my walk.' Consequently The Binns house today has the look of a fort about it.

Folklore further averred that General Tam regularly played cards with the Devil. On one occasion when the General won the Devil threw the table upon which they had been playing out of the window into a nearby stretch of water known as Sergeant's Pond. When the pool was drained in 1878 a heavy table of carved marble was found in the mud at the bottom of the pool.

Bladnoch, Dumfries & Galloway   GHOST

The River Bladnoch gives its name to the village not far from Wigtown. The village is remembered in folklore for its ruined Baldoon Castle, the haunt of Janet Dalrymple.

Janet Dalrymple was the eldest daughter of the lawyer Sir James Dalrymple, later 1st Viscount Stair (1619–95), and his wife, the formidable Margaret Ross of Balneel. Janet, it is said, was forced by her parents to marry David Dunbar, heir of Sir David Dunbar of Baldoon. Her own choice for a husband was

Archibald, 3rd Lord Rutherford. Folklorists have three basic versions of the ensuing story to choose from after Janet's marriage to David Dunbar in the Kirk of Old Luce, near to the old Dalrymple home of Carsecleugh Castle. Version one said that Janet stabbed her new bridegroom on their wedding night and died of a hysterical fit, the second says that David Dunbar stabbed Janet to be discovered next morning a raving lunatic, while the third has the spurned Lord Rutherford entering the bridal chamber to stab Dunbar to death.

Sir Walter Scott took the basic story, applied his lawyer's mind to the versions, and immortalised it in his *The Bride of Lammermoor* (1819). He has his character Lucy Ashton (as Janet) forced to marry Frank Hayston, Laird of Bucklaw (as David Dunbar). Sir Walter's version of the scene in Janet Dunbar's bridal chamber goes like this:

> *The bridal feast was followed by dancing. The bride and bridegroom retired as usual, when of a sudden the most wild and piercing cries were heard from the nuptial chamber. It was then the custom, to prevent any coarse peasantry which old times perhaps admitted, that the key to the nuptial chamber should be entrusted to the bridesman. He was called upon, but refused at first to give it up, till the shrieks became so hideous that he was compelled to hasten with others to learn the cause. On opening the door, they found the bridegroom lying across the threshold, dreadfully wounded, and streaming with blood. The bride was then sought for. She was found in the corner of the large chimney, having no covering save her shift, and that dabbled in gore. There she said grinning at them, mopping and mowing, as I heard the expression used; in a word absolutely insane. The only words she spoke were, 'Take up your bonny bridegroom.'*

In reality Janet Dalrymple died on 12 September 1669 some two weeks after her marriage; Lord Rutherford died unmarried in 1685. Local folklore recounts how Janet Dalrymple was to be seen for many decades after her family home had been ruined walking spectrally amongst the stones 'mopping and mowing' as Sir Walter had described. Others aver that what happened in the bridal chamber that night was brought about by the Devil – he had been taunting Dunbar and Janet had attacked him with a knife, the Devil had stepped aside and Janet's blow had accidentally killed her new husband.

Bodesbeck, Dumfries & Galloway   FAIRYLORE

The farm at Bodesbeck lies some six miles north-east of Moffat, near to the 2,173-foot-high Bodesbeck Law. It is perhaps *the* place in Scotland to be traditionally associated with a 'brownie', the most industrious of Scotland's folkloric creatures.

The labours of the brownie made Bodesbeck the most affluent and well-kept farm in the Borders as the creature toiled, usually at night, at sheep-marking, hay-stooking, peat-stacking and the like. Everyone knew that brownies only worked for their food as payment, morsels that they selected themselves from larder and dairy. One year, when the farm had gathered a particularly good harvest, the farmer left out an increased food supply for the brownie. The creature was insulted at what it took to be a slight – no brownie expected extra payment for extra work – so one morning the farm labourers came to the farm to see that none of the usual tasks had been done, and as they stood disappointedly they saw the brownie walking away across the fields, and as he went he sang:

Ca' Brownie ca',	call
A' the luck o' Bodesbeck	all
Awa' tae Leithen Ha'.	away to … Hall

James Hogg, the Ettrick Shepherd, wrote of the Brownie of Bodesbeck in an eponymous long tale in 1818. In this he identified the brownie as a person, John Brown of Caldwell.

Brackley, Argyll   CURING STONE

In Gaelic this stone is known as *Carraig an Talaidh* (the Stone of the Lulling), but it is also spoken of as the Refuge Stone, or the Toothache Stone. This chambered cairn inspired a local legend that it could cure toothache if the sufferer drove a nail into it at midnight. Several nails can be seen in the cairn's stones.

Bridge of Don, Grampian SUPERSTITION

The Auld Brig o' Balgownie, bynamed the 'Auld Brig o' Don', spans 62 feet. across the River Don at Old Aberdeen. It was built by Henry Le Cheyn, Bishop of Aberdeen (d.1328) and became associated with a curious superstition:

> *Brig o' Balgownie, wight's your wa'*   stout is your wall
> *Wi' a wife's ae son an' a mear's ae foal*
> *Down ye shall fa'.*

The inference was that if it was crossed by a woman's only son, or a mare's only foal – or both at the same time – the bridge would fall. George Gordon, 6th Baron Byron (1788–1824) alludes to the superstition in his *Don Juan* (1819) in Canto X, verse 18. He describes the bridge's 'black wall' (he misquotes the verse superstition with 'black' instead of 'wight') and adds the note: 'I still remember, though perhaps I may misquote, the awful proverb which made me pause to cross it, and yet lean over it with a childish delight, being an only son, at least by the mother's side.'

Burghead, Morayshire CUSTOM

With its fine views over the Moray Firth, the fishing village of Burghead was fortified by the Picts and the Norsemen, whose rituals and beliefs may be reflected in the annual custom of 'Burning the Clavie'.

On 11 January a 'clavie' is constructed from a sawn-in-half tar barrel mounted on a six-foot salmon-fisherman's pole, called a spoke. The clavie's fuel is broken staves of a herring cask and tarred wood. A flaming peat ignites the clavie which is processed around the streets of Burghead to a hill called the Doorie. Here the clavie fire is augmented with more wood. Remnant blazing embers are scattered down the Doorie, where people gather a personal ember for good luck as a talisman against evil spirits for a year.

Folklorists link the clavie custom to the mid-winter fires of the *Druides* and the fire-worship of the Norsemen whose petitioner bonfires begged the sun to return.

C

Castleton, Roxburghshire, Borders WIZARD

Nine Stane Rig Stone Circle and Hermitage Castle are entwined in Scottish folklore because of their association with William de Soulis, Lord of Liddesdale, and Hereditary Butler of Scotland. De Soulis was one of the prominent aristocrats of the early years of Scotland's struggle for independence which followed the death of Alexander III in 1286. As a larger-than-life character, de Soulis's reputation built up into a folkloric story that cut across historical fact.

De Soulis's Border base was Hermitage Castle by the Hermitage Water, built around 1244 by Walter Comyn, Earl of Mentieth. From here de Soulis is said to have terrorised the district for years, and local legend has it that he murdered Richard Knut of Kielder around 1289. Knut was deemed to be protected with a 'magic suit of armour', so de Soulis was said to have used magic powers to vanquish him. Slowly de Soulis entered the people's blacklist of supposed wizards. In time, too, he was credited with a familiar – an evil spirit – called Robin Redcap.

Folktale further recounted how Redcap had assured de Soulis that he could not be harmed by steel or hemp; thus he was safe from hanging or death by iron weapons.

In reality de Soulis was arrested for treason and spent the rest of his life in captivity, dying in Dumbarton Castle, but this was not good enough for local balladists, and they formulated a more bloody end for the tyrant of their folklore.

As a consequence of Redcap's prophecy de Soulis was to prove impervious to the ropes and billhooks of the frustrated Liddesdale peasantry whom he is said to have persecuted, so following the advice of Thomas of Ercildoun they captured him, rolled him in a piece of lead sheeting and boiled him in a cauldron at the Nine Stane Rig Stone Circle, east of Hermitage Castle.

Dr John Leyden, a keen folklorist and friend of Sir Walter Scott, collected these verses on the fate of de Soulis for Scott's *Minstrelsy of the Scottish Border* (1802–03):

> *On a circle of stones they placed the pot,*
> *On a circle of stones but barely nine;*
> *They heated it red and fiery hot,*
> *And the burnished brass did glimmer and shine.*

> *They rolled him up in a sheet of lead –*
> *A sheet of lead for a funeral pall;*
> *They plunged him into a cauldron red,*
> *And melted him body, lead, bones and all.*

Channelkirk, Berwickshire, Borders   FOLK HERO

Although bearing a Saxon name, Cuthbert the Shepherd was born around 637 somewhere near where the southern slopes of the Moorfoot Hills meet the Lammermuirs in the parish of Channelkirk. In those days it was at the northern tip of the Kingdom of Northumbria.

While tending his flocks in Lauderdale by the Well of the Holy Water Cleuch, Cuthbert saw a vision in the skies above the Lammermuirs. Therein he was given a direction to pursue a holy life and he made his way to the now vanished monastery of Old Mailros, which had been founded by Bishop Aidan of Lindisfarne. Here he entered the holy life to become one of the most famous of all the northern church-men as Abbot-Bishop of Lindisfarne (Holy Island). His shrine at Durham Cathedral was to be one of the most celebrated in Christendom and Cuthbert became a folklore icon as a healer and missionary.

The feathers of the eider ducks of Lindisfarne (St Cuthbert's Ducks) and the shells from Holy Island beach were all common talismans in the Scottish Borders throughout medieval history, and churches were dedicated to him from Kirkcudbright to Coldingham. The story of Cuthbert's transformation from shepherd to bishop was a popular one amongst Scotland's wandering balladeers.

Chirnside, Berwickshire, Borders   FOLK THEME

In the graveyard of Chirnside's old parish church is the tomb of the Rev. Henry Erskine, minister of the parish, who married as his second wife the Orcadian Margaret Halcrow in 1674. When Margaret died she was buried with a magnificent five-diamond cluster ring. As she was put in her coffin, the undertaker and grave-digger John Carr took a fancy to the ring and decided to retrieve it. On the day of the funeral Carr pretended that it was too late on in the day and the ground too wet to fill in her grave properly, and he returned to the cemetery during the night. He found that Margaret's finger had swollen and he could not remove the ring, so he began to cut the finger with his pocket-knife. To his horror, Margaret sat up and screamed; she had been in some kind of coma and the flowing of the blood had revived her.

Back at the manse the Rev. Erskine was inconsolable at his loss and was looking forlornly out of the window. He could hardly believe his eyes when he saw Margaret, clad in her shroud, approaching the front door and waving to him with 'Let me in, let me in, I'm fair clemmed wi' the cauld.' Erskine died in 1696; Margaret herself died in 1716 to be buried at Scotland Well, Stirlingshire. The story of Margaret Erskine became a folklore theme to be cannibalised with different names and different locations.

Conon Bridge, Ross & Cromarty   ANIMALS

A village popular with anglers and flanked by 3,429-foot Ben Wyves, Conon Bridge and its associated River Conon brings into Scottish folklore the otter as a supernatural beast. The otter does not appear much in British folklore but at Conon Bridge they talked about the King Otter. Should you catch one – and the beast is lighter and larger than others – you would be granted one wish to secure its freedom.

Alternatively a warrior could become impervious to swords, arrows and bullets if he wore the King Otter's pelt. In this area, also, burns were soothed by rubbing them with a (black) otter's tongue. The River Conon figured too as the haunt of a *kelpie* (water-horse).

Corrievreckan, Argyllshire   WHIRLPOOL

The Strait of Corrievreckan lies between the islands of Scarba and Jura and contains Breccan's Cauldron. Known on charts as Corrievreckan, folklore has it that one Breccan perished here when his fleet of fifty ships was sucked into the whirlpool in the sixth century. At a later date his kinsman St Columba made a safe passage past Corrievreckan, and as he did so a hand rose from the whirlpool bearing a rib-bone of Breccan.

Cortachy, Angus   GHOST/MUSIC

Airlie Castle, the former traditional home of the Earls of Airlie at Cortachy, was the scene of what folklore calls 'supernatural music'. The lore concerns the Airlie Drummer and it dates from 1640 when Airlie Castle was captured by the Earl of Argyll and his Covenanters and was burned to a shell. One of the garrison who defended the castle was a drummer of the Cameron clan. He was blamed for not alerting the Ogilvie defenders of the coming attack and they left him to die in the flames. Since that time the ghostly Airlie Drummer gave warning of the death of the head of the Ogilvie family, the Earls of Airlie.

In her memoirs, *Thatched with Gold* (1962), Mabell, Countess of Airlie, noted how the drummer was heard at the death of the 8th Earl in 1881 and attested by Lady Margaret Cameron, Lady Dalkeith and the Countess of Lathom. He beat a tattoo again, said Lady Airlie, when the 9th Earl died at the Battle of Diamond Hill in the Boer War of 1899–1902.

There is no more emotive place in the folklore of Scottish Jacobitism than the field of Culloden where, on the 16 April 1746, the well-fed, well-armed, refreshed soldiers of Prince William Augustus, Duke of Cumberland, defeated the tired, hungry, demoralised troops of his kinsman, Prince Charles Edward Stuart. Apart from the well-known Jacobite associations, there is one more link for the site with Scottish folklore. The lore of the old Scots phrase 'The Nine of Diamonds is the Curse of Scotland' says that it was upon this playing card that the Duke of Cumberland wrote his order for the slaying of the Jacobites vanquished after the battle. Others said that the 'Curse' was associated with the Massacre of Glencoe of 1692. Early in his reign William III summoned all the Scottish clan chiefs to take an oath of allegiance. The Macdonalds failed to do so. Because of a misunderstanding a warrant was issued for the punishment of the Macdonalds and their hereditary enemies the Campbells carried it out. Some said that the then Secretary of State, Sir John Dalrymple of Stair, used the nine of diamonds for his signature, agreeing to the massacre.

There's more to Culloden Moor than its fame as the site of the last battle fought on British soil. For decades on the first Sunday in May, folk have trysted at the Cloutie Well in memory of a pagan water-cult. Known sometimes a *Tobar n'Oige* (Well of Youth), or St Mary's Well, the Cloutie Well takes it more prosaic name from the custom of hanging *clouts* (rags) by the well to 'fix' a wish. Drinking the water of the well was always preceded by walking sunwise round the well three times in respect and the casting in of a coin for good luck. The significance of the rags? – In pagan times devotees would take off their outer garments before petitioning the gods.

The old rhyme was quite specific:

> *Twixt Wigtown and the town of Ayr*
> *Portpatrick and the Cruives of Cree,*
> *No man may think for to bide there*
> *Unless he court St Kennedie.*

The 'saint' mentioned was the nickname for the Kennedy family who were lairds of Culzean Castle having acquired it from the Earls of Carrick. Beneath the castle the Caves of Culzean were long identified as rendezvous for fairy folk at Hallowe'en, and these creatures have a mention in the history of the Kennedys, Earls of Cassilis, concerning the rescue of one of the family.

As Culzean has been associated with the Kennedys since the fourteenth century, an old ballad ties in one of the early lairds of the estate with the defeat of the Flemings by the French in 1382 – the laird had been fishing in Flanders as a mercenary. The tale begins some years before when the laird met a small boy with a wooden pitcher who begged that he might give him some ale for his sick mother. The laird agreed and sent the boy to his butler with the instruction that the pitcher be filled.

The butler held the pitcher to a half-full ale barrel's tap. When the barrel was empty the small pitcher was still not full. Fearing the wrath of the laird should he not carry out his instructions the butler opened another barrel. He had hardly begun to turn the tap when the pitcher began to overflow. Not a words of thanks did the boy offer as he walked away to his mother with the ale.

The next scene of the tale is Flanders and the laird is just hours away from being executed by the French for helping the Flemings. As he waits in his cell he is amazed to see the boy who had asked for the ale materialise in his cell. In a trice the boy had broken the laird's chains, lifted the laird onto his shoulders and flew him back to Culzean. Thus was the sudden arrival of the laird back to his home accounted for and all through the gratitude of a Fairy Boy.

D

Dale, Shetland FABULOUS BEAST

Scottish folklore developed its own menagerie of fabulous beasts, so the mention of a more international creature of this kind is rare in local tales. At Dale, three miles north-west of Lerwick, a Shetland woman is said to have discovered the egg of a cockatrice which she placed under one of her hens to hatch. The creature hatched, ate the hen's chicks and made its home in a pile of peat.

The cockatrice enters folklore and heraldry as a beast with the wings of a fowl, tail of a dragon and the head of a cockerel. It takes its name from being fabulously produced from a seven-year-old cock's spherical egg, fertilised by a dragon when the dog star Sirius was in the ascendant, and hatched by a toad.

To look at the beast directly in the eye was to cause instant death. For this reason the creature was also called a basilisk. As Edmund Spenser (*c.*1552–99) wrote in *The Faerie Queene*:

> *The Basilisk*
> *From powerful eyes close venim doth convey*
> *Into the looker's heart, and killeth far away.*

As to the fate of the Dale cockatrice, Shetland lore advised that it could only be destroyed by flames, so the pile of peat in which it lived was set on fire and the beast perished.

Dalgety Bay, Fife FOLK BALLAD

The old estate of Donibristle once stretched from St Davids Harbour on the Firth of Forth, to the bounds of Aberdour, and is still remembered in three local place names and Donibristle Bay, a western part of modern Dalgety Bay. Local tradition has it that the earliest Donibristle House was the seat of the abbots of the Augustinian abbey on the island of Inchcolm. This became the property of Sir James Stewart of Beath, 1st Lord Doune, commendator of the old ecclesiastical properties and father of the hero of the folk ballad 'The Bonny Earl o' Moray'.

> *Ye Highlands and ye Lowlands*
> *Oh, whare hae ye been?*
> *They hae slain the Earl o' Moray*
> *And lain him on the green.*

The 'Bonny Earl' was James Stewart (b.1568) who married Elizabeth the elder daughter of the royal bastard also called James Stewart, Earl of Moray, Regent of Scotland. Folklore talks of the young earl as handsome and he is described as being in the great favour of Queen Anne, husband of King James VI who it was said was not happy about the uxorial infatuation:

> *He was a braw gallant*
> *And he rade at the ring;*
> *And the bonnie Earl o' Moray –*
> *Oh! he might hae been a king …*

> *He was a braw gallant,*
> *And he play'd at the glove;*
> *And the bonnie Earl o' Moray*
> *Oh! he was the Queen's luve.*

Moray's mortal enemy was George Gordon, Earl of Huntly (1563–1636); while Moray was the flower of the Protestant Party, Huntly was leader of the Catholic Party, and when he married into the Morays the 'Bonny Earl' took on the feud hatreds between his in-laws and the Huntlys. History points to the political aspects of Moray's death, with the collusion of the king, while the folk ballad dwells on the romantic.

Huntly arrived at Donibristle, besieged the house and called upon Moray to surrender. He refused and Huntly's followers set fire to the house. Under the cover of a feint supplied by Dunbar, Sheriff of Moray, the 'Bonny Earl' made his escape from the house, but was soon discovered hiding in the rocks along Donibristle Bay, Moray was slain and entered folklore as a 'braw, braw gallant':

> *Oh! lang will his lady*
> *Look fraw the castle doune*
> *Ere she see the Earl o'Moray*
> *Come sounding through the town.*

Superstitious folk felt that Donibristle House was doomed; although it was rebuilt, it burned down again in 1858, and the whole area was sold in the sixties for the new town of Dalgety Bay.

Dalrymple, Ayrshire GIPSYLORE

On the banks of the River Doon, Dalrymple lies five miles north of Maybole. Here the poet Robert Burns went to school for a while to improve his writing. It is also the location of a folkloric tale which like many another denied reality. The folklore concerns Jean, daughter of Thomas Hamilton, 1st Earl of Haddington, and first wife of John, 6th Earl of Cassilis (d.1668). It is said that when her husband was away at the Westminster Assembly of the Long Parliament of King Charles II, Lady Jean took up with her former lover, the handsome gypsy John Faa. Her story is told in the folk ballad 'The Gypsy Laddie':

> *The gypsies they cam' to Lord Casillis' yett*   gate
> *And oh, but they sang bonnie.*
> *They sang saw sweet, and sae complete,*
> *That down came our fair Ladie.*
>
> *She cam' tripping down the stairs,*
> *With a' her maids before her.*
> *As soon as they saw the weel-far'd face*
> *They caste their glamourie owre her*   charm over

For her infidelity Lord Cassilis is said to have put his wife under house arrest at Maybole for the rest of her life. The dates for the story don't fit; the Westminster Assembly took place in 1643 and Jean died in 1642, and surviving letters show the respect in which Lord Cassilis held his wife. However the folktale persisted.

Duns, Berwickshire, Borders

Set on the north-eastern slopes of Cockburn Law, in the parish of Duns, by Abbey St Bathans, is the fort and broch (an Iron Age circular building of unusually thick walls) of Edin's Hall.

Here in Border folktale dwelt the Giant Etin, who daily plundered the surrounding farms. He was regularly to be seen with a stolen bull on his shoulders and a sheep under each arm. From time to time people who dwelt in the surrounding hills went missing and it was believed that the giant had captured them as slaves. The pebble (a two-ton boulder) which Etin tipped from his shoe is still pointed out in the Whiteadder Water.

What made the giant different in Scottish folklore was that he had three heads. Many had tried to lure him to his death but none had succeeded, until three young men (two of which were brothers), sons of two widows, tried their luck. The boys were to make their attempts separately, and the lot fell to one of the brothers to go first. Before he set off he gave his brother a treasured knife with the warning that if it should stay bright he was safe, but should it rust he was in danger.

The lad made his way into the hills above the Whiteadder and encountered a shepherd. Enquiring as to the owner of the sheep he was told they belonged to the giant; a tyrant who could only be slain with one blow of a double-headed axe. The boy went on until he came to the giant's broch home. He entered to discover the giant at supper.

In a mellow mood the giant sought for entertainment and began to ask the boy questions concerning Scottish history. Enraged that the boy could answer none of the questions the giant smote him with a wooden mallet and turned him into stone.

Back at home the remaining brother noticed that his sibling's knife had dimmed with rust. Despite his mother's protestations the boy set off into the hills to pursue his brother. Exactly the same fate awaited him and the giant set the two petrified boys on each side of his fireplace as ornaments on which to knock out his pipe.

When the second brother failed to return the third remaining boy took to the road in search of them. On the road up into the hills he encountered a poor woman sitting by the Whiteadder. He shared his supper with her and she told him much about Scotland's history. From a bag she had beside her she withdrew a bundle and gave it to the boy with the instruction that he was only to open it if he was in danger.

The boy reached the giant's broch and was pulled inside by the hungry ogre. He had had a poor day at the hunt and the boy, he said, would be just the right size to fill his bannock. For his entertainment the giant asked the boy the questions about Scottish History that he had asked the other boys. This time, because of what the old woman had told him, the boy answered correctly. The giant was puzzled but reaching for his knife made to slit the boy's throat in preparation for his supper. The boy remembered the bundle the old woman had given him, so he dodged the giant and pulled the sacking away to reveal a double-headed axe. Wielding it easily the boy severed the giant's three heads with one blow. As if by magic the two petrified brothers were restored to flesh and from cupboards all around came forth Border folk who had been missing for years.

Dornoch, Sutherland, Highlands WITCH

A royal burgh and old county town, in which was located the seat of the old bishops of Caithness, Dornoch enters the pages of Scotland's blacker folklore by being the place where the last judicial execution for witchcraft took place.

The year was 1727 – despite the date of 1722 being given on a stone in a cottage garden by the Links – and two impoverished Highland women were accused of witchcraft, tried and condemned to be executed by fire. The younger of the two women escaped from prison but the older one perished. Her name is given as Janet Horne and she is accused 'of having ridden upon her own daughter, transformed into a pony and shod by the Devil'. Records show that even into the 1790s the relatives of Janet Horne were shunned by credulous locals.

Durness, Sutherland, Highlands   WIZARD

Flanked by the Kyle of Durness and Loch Eriboll, Durness is famous for its nearby three-chambered Smoo' Cave and it associations with the landowner Donald Mackay, 4th Lord Reay (d.1761), known in folklore as the 'Wizard of Reay'. A well-travelled aristocrat, Reay is said to have studied the black arts in Italy and was an acolyte of the Devil. One day, it seems, Reay was exploring the Smoo' Cave when he encountered the Devil. Reay by this time had renounced his supposed allegiance and in a fit of anger the Devil blasted his way out of the cave. This is thought to be how the aperture was made in the Smoo' Cave through which the Smoo' Burn enters.

E

Edinburgh   AMULETS AND TALISMANS

Once Edinburgh was the centre for 'lucky jewellery', as well as amulets and talismans. An amulet may be described as an object which is believed to have a beneficial influence on the owner. A talisman is specially constructed with a particular purpose in mind, often with an incantation or spell incorporated on it at the most propitious time.

Craftsmen made such items in Scotland from at least the Bronze Age (1900 BC–500 BC) and archaeologists are regularly digging them up. These charms are usually associated with the elements of fire, earth, water and air. The golden age for making such items, however, was the Middle Ages, as many such charms were used by those on pilgrimage or to buy at the shrine of a particular saint. Thus the medieval burgh kirk of St Giles (now St Giles Cathedral), Edinburgh, did a roaring trade in medallions showing the saint, patron saint of cripples.

Outside the kirk of St Giles were to be found the lean-to covered lock-up stalls, the Luckenbooths (demolished 1817), of several Edinburgh silversmiths, who made the famous Luckenbooth Brooches as tokens of good luck and for lovers' gifts. Usually these were of engraved silver in the shape of a heart, or two hearts entwined.

Many of these Edinburgh charms were passed down from generation to generation. Others were magic heirlooms. One such was the Brooch of Lorne, said to have been made from a jewel lost by Robert I, the Bruce, in battle.

Ednam, Roxburghshire, Borders   FAIRY MUSIC

The birthplace of James Thomson (1700–48), author of 'Rule Britannia' and 'The Seasons', and Henry Francis Lyte (1793–1847), versifier of the hymn 'Abide with Me', the age-old village of Ednam, some two and a half miles north of Kelso, is famed in folklore also for another type of composition.

A little to the west of the village is the Pictish burial mound known in local parlance as the Piper's Knowe. Local folk believed that an Ednam piper entered the hillock to learn the secrets of fairy music, for here locals said the fairies had an encampment. Alas, the piper forgot to take a protective amulet with him and he was unable to find his way out again. From time to time his mournful pipes were heard as he paced up and down within the knowe.

Eildon Hills, Borders   KING ARTHUR

The bifurcated Eildon Hills, split in a moment by the wizard Michael Scot, the superstitious say, lie between the Bowden Burn and the River Tweed as the latter snakes past Melrose and Newstead (the Roman *Trimontium*) towards St Boswells. They are rich in Border folklore. As Sir Walter Scott said: 'I can stand on the Eildon Hills and point out forty-three places famous in war and verse.' The hills though are most celebrated in folklore for their association with King Arthur.

Sometime at the beginning of the nineteenth century, a horse *couper* (dealer) called Richard Stewart used to visit regularly the horse markets in the villages around the Eildons. A jolly, rumbustuous fellow; he was known as Canonbie Dick, after his home village by the Esk in Dumfriesshire. On one occasion Dick was crossing Bowden Moor, around the west side of the Eildons, with a string of horses he had bought, when he encountered a stranger. Dick peered at the stranger through the encircling evening gloom and noted that he was dressed in the clothes that were long out of fashion and that he spoke with a refined tongue. The stranger had taken a fancy to the horses Dick was leading and offered him a price for them on the spot. As it was far in excess of what Dick had paid for them, he accepted. Counting the coins as the stranger rode away with his horses, Dick noticed that the pieces were all of antique minting but his teeth confirmed that they were pure gold.

The horse dealer was to meet the stranger on subsequent occasions to sell more horses for gold. On one particular occasion the stranger invited Dick back to his home for a drink to seal their current bargain. Anxious to find out more about his customer Dick accepted, and they rode into the Eildons as far as the old witch meeting place of Lucken Hare Rock. As they entered an opening in the hill the stranger saw that Dick was dubious. He smiled: 'You are more than welcome to come into my abode. But if you are afraid of what you see there, you will regret it for ever.'

The thought of the imminent drink spurred Canonbie Dick to nod to the stranger that he was not afraid and they rode deep into the hill. At length the passage widened to a huge cavern, and as Dick's eyes became used to the semi-darkness he saw the high-roofed chamber was stacked with antique armour, a row of stalls with horses in them and a parallel row of catafalques upon which lay, in full armour, a row of somnolent knights.

As Dick walked passed them with the stranger he wondered at the complete silence of the place. They approached a table upon which lay a hunting horn and a sword. Motioning for Dick to sit down, the stranger poured a drink from a large ewer and sat down opposite to him. Looking directly into his face the stranger said to Dick: 'Whosoever can draw this sword and blow this horn will be King of Britain. But they must be drawn and blown in the right order.'

Dick realised that he was being given the chance to choose. Believing he had nothing to lose Dick reached for the horn first and gave it an echoing call. In a moment the cavern was flooded with light, the knights awoke and each sprang up to take their places by their steeds. Dick made to snatch up the sword, but from far away in the rock roof above him a voice thundered:

Woe to the coward that ever he was born
Who did not draw the sword before he blew the horn.

At once a huge tempest blew through the chamber and Dick found himself swept out of the cavern and onto the open hillside.

Dick lay stunned on the hillside for a long time in the sunshine. Later two shepherds found him and carried him down to Melrose. As his senses came back to him Dick recounted what had happened and what he had seen. Most folk who heard him mocked at his credulity or slated him as a liar, but one old man quietened the company when he said that during his youth he had heard how King Arthur and his Knights still slept under the Eildon Hills. They were waiting for the call that would bring them riding forth to battle with the powers of oppression. It had all been foretold by True Thomas of Ercildoun, who had the task of buying fresh horses for the knights with a payment of gold pieces from Arthur's treasury.

Elderslie, Strathclyde   FOLK HERO

Where historical facts start to fade folklore begins, and the legends behind the life of William Wallace were stimulated in the public eye and given a new airing by the 1995 film *Braveheart*. Thus Elderslie, the old Renfrewshire town once known for its carpet manufacture, was given centre stage as the probable birthplace of Wallace around 1272. A monument in the town is set near to the folk hero's supposed actual birthplace.

In reality little is known for sure about the life of Wallace. Historical and folklore perspective now underline the dramatic events of Scotland's history of independence as beginning around Dundee. When Edward I imposed the puppet king John Balliol on Scotland and coerced the Guardians of Scotland to surrender their power bases to him Wallace's father Sir Malcolm Wallace was forced to flee from Elderslie and take up residence with relations at Kilspindie in the Carse of Gowrie, near Dundee. Wallace is said to attended the then monastic Dundee High School. There he met his future biographer John Blair. Yet most of the romance and folklore roots concerning Wallace came from the account of his life by travelling storyteller Blind Harry, who made Wallace into a kind of Robin Hood and a national hero.

Wallace soon found himself at odds with the English garrison at Dundee, and he fought with Selby, the son of the city's English governor. Folklore says Wallace fled to a house in Dundee's Overgate where he was sheltered, disguised as a lass at a spinning wheel. He fled back to Kilspindie, pausing to eat a meal at Longforgan. Dundee Museum still has a stone kirn on which, says the folktale, Wallace sat to eat his repast.

Wallace now disappeared from history, and folklore records he formed a band of guerrillas to fight for Scotland's freedom. Again he appears as a thorn in the flesh of the Dundee garrison in the 1290s. Wallace became the only effective leader of armed resistance to English rule in Scotland. On 11 September 1296 he defeated the English army at the Battle of Stirling, but finally Wallace was crushingly routed at Falkirk in 1298 and was executed at London for treason in 1305.

History shows that many of Wallace's contemporaries could have become national heroes like him, but he it was who pushed the Scots into determined unity and fired their imagination as to what could be done. Folklore did the rest.

Elie, Fife   VANISHED HAMLET

Along with Earlsferry, into which it now merges, the sixteenth-century Burgh of Barony of Elie was a favourite summer resort. Its environs are seeped in history, for at the royal burgh of Earlsferry, boatmen took Macduff, Earl of Fife across the Firth of Forth to safety when he was fleeing the wrath of Macbeth. For decades, too, the folk would scour the beaches for 'Elie rubies' (small, garnets) to keep them for their healing properties. Just to the north of Elie stands Elie House which was begun in 1697. One famous occupant was to add to the folklore of the place.

Janet Fall was the second daughter of Charles Fall, Provost of Dunbar. A descendant of the gypsy Faas, she was the famous Jenny Faa mentioned by Scottish historian and essayist Thomas Carlyle (1795–1881), as being 'a coquette and a beauty'. In 1750 she married Sir John Anstruther and immediately impressed her personality on the neighbourhood of Elie. Still today locals point out Lady's Tower at Elie Ness; this was Lady Janet's summer-house from which she would emerge to sea bathe. Whenever she want to bathe a bellman would walk through the streets of Elie to warn of her intentions and for the locals to stay away.

Because of her gypsy connections it is said that Lady Janet built up a dislike for the hamlet of Balclevie which stood within the Elie estate. The hamlet was inhabited by tinker-gypsies and may have reminded her of her lowly ancestry, so she nagged her husband to have the hamlet removed 'to improve the view' and the inhabitants were dispossessed.

It is believed that the eviction inspired Sir Walter Scott to weave the actuality around the fictitious eviction of the gypsies from Derncleuch by the Laird of Ellangowan in his novel *Guy Mannering* (1815). Indeed local legend had it that a *speywife* (fortune-teller) from the doomed Balclevie had cursed the Anstruthers for what had been done (just as Meg Merrilees cursed Ellangowan in Scott's book) and forecast that only six generations of Anstruthers would live in Elie House; the prognostication was proved true.

Eriskay, Outer Hebrides JACOBITE

Although there were Jacobite risings in 1708, which failed through bad luck, in 1715, which foundered in incompetence, and in 1719 because it was too small, it was that of 1745 which gave the Jacobites – the followers of King James VII & II – their place in Scottish legend, and the roots of Scottish Jacobite folklore are to be found on the beach at Eriskay.

Prince Charles Edward Stuart – grandson of James VII & II – landed on Eriskay on 23 July 1745 from the French vessel *Du Teillay* with Scoto-Hibernian-French followers, with the intention of winning back the throne of Great Britain for the Stuarts in the person of his father Prince James Francis Edward Stuart the putative King James VIII & III. Today the folklore begins on the dunes of the island, between Barra and South Uist, for there the pink convolvulus grows, brought in seed by Charles Edward Stuart from France. A focal point for the seeds of the surrounding Jacobite folklore, though, was placed in 1995 in the form of a cairn to commemorate the famous landing at *Coilleag a' Phrionnsa* (Prince's Strand).

Eskdalemuir, Dumfries & Galloway   CUSTOM

At the junction of roads to Dumfries, Lockerbie and Langholm, Eskdalemuir stands in the valley of the White Esk. Here at the junction of the Black Esk and the White Esk was the site of the annual Handfasting Fair, where young folk paired off for a year's 'trial marriage'. If all went well (and the girl got pregnant) they would wed by the next year's fair. Sometimes if the two were incompatible, the offspring went to the father's family to be raised as second to his legitimate heirs. No stigma attached to the woman. It is said that when Eskdale belonged to the Cistercian monks of Melrose Abbey that the abbot would take a note of the 'pairings' and subsequently regularise the marriages. Some folklorists say that the root of the custom is in the pagan feast of Lug (Lugnasad – Lammas) when promiscuous couplings took place.

Folkloric records aver too, that King Robert II (1316–90) was engaged in such a handfasting ceremony with Elizabeth Muire, and that John of Carrick was their handfast child who became King Robert III (1337–1406). The custom went into desuetude all over Scotland after the Reformation.

Between the island of Rousay and mainland Orkney lies the Eynhallow Sound and the lost settlement of Eynhallow on the eponymous islet; the ruins of its Benedictine monastic church can still be made out. Once the folk of Eynhallow, the old stories told, were in communion with the Fin People of Finfolkaheen, a twin community beneath the waves of the South. During each summer the Fin People – half fish and half human – would bask on the shore near Eynhallow village. Both Fin-Men and Fin-Women would endeavour to woo human lovers. If they were successful in seducing a human the Fin People lost their fish characteristics so that they could live on land.

Eynhallow was believed to have the capability of becoming invisible from time to time, mostly to save it from seaborne marauders. Stories of habitations that disappear and reappear are quite common in the folklore of the northern Scottish islands. The dramatist Sir James Matthew Barrie (1860–1937) used the folklore as a basis for his play *Mary Rose* (1920).

F

Fitful Head, Shetland   DEMONIC HORSE

The 928-foot Fitful Head, some three miles south-west of Dunrossness, was given literary fame as the home of the prophetess Norna in Sir Walter Scott's *The Pirate* (1821). Not for nothing was Scott enchanted by its atmosphere, for here folklore says lived, in a cave in its side, the savage being called Black Eric. From here he rode out on his demon seahorse, Tangie, to raid and harry the surrounding crofts. The cave is still known as the Thief's Hole.

At length one courageous crofter, Sandy Breamer, had had enough of Black Eric and cornered him at the top of the Head. The savage sheep-stealer fell to his death in the sea, but Tangie continued to terrorise the district for a while in his attempts to secure a mortal bride.

This story is undoubtedly a folk memory of one of the

tales of the Aesir horsemen, the followers of the Norse God Odin. The source books of Nordic myths, the *Eddas*, were always careful to list the Aesir's horses from Alsuid and Arvar, steeds of the sun god, to Sleipnir, the mount of Odin himself.

Forfar, Angus   WITCHES

Forfar Museum contains the famous 'Witch Bridle'. This was the iron gag worn by seventeenth-century 'witches' on their way to execution. The populace were afraid that witches would curse them on the way to the stake so the condemned were locked in the bridle for the journey; thus suffered Helen Guthrie in 1661.

Forres, Moray, Grampian   WITCHES

King Duncan I (1034–40) often held court at Forres. On their way to Forres, Macbeth and Banquo were reputed to have met, on the 'blasted heath', the 'weird sisters' of Shakespeare's play. At Forres is the Witches' Stone marking the spot of the executions of Isobel Elder and Isabel Simson in 1663.

Fortingall, Perthshire, Tayside   FOLK LEGEND

Pontius Pilate is chiefly known to us for ordering the execution of Jesus of Nazareth. Yet the little hamlet of Fortingall, on the River Lyon, some eight miles west-south-west of Aberfeldy, is still mentioned in folklore as Pontius Pilate's birthplace.

The old folktale states that Pontius Pilate's father was an ambassador sent to Scotland on a peace embassy by Caesar Augustus. His mission was to parley with Metallanus, King of the Caledonians (from whom the Menzies clan claim descent), who was then at Dun Gael fort, Balnacraig by Fortingall. It was during this tour of duty, the legend has it, that Pontius Pilate was born sometime in the late years of the first century BC.

Nothing is known for certain before AD 26 of Pontius Pilate's background and career. We know that he was a soldier and procurator. It is likely, too, that he came from Roman equestrian stock (that is the middle classes), and his name *Pontius Pileatus* supports the suggestion of him coming from northern Italy.

The historian Raphael Holinshed, writing in the sixteenth century, tells us that Emperor Caesar August (63 BC – AD 14) did send ambassadors to Britain, but the camp near Fortingall said to be Pontius Pilate's birthplace was of a very much later date. Also, the Romans did not penetrate Scotland until after 79 AD, so it is very unlikely that Roman ambassadors were talking to Scottish tribesmen before AD 83.

The story has all the hallmarks of a piece of Scottish folk romance – some hazy historical details grafted onto a local tradition – but where did the tradition come from? It is likely to be a Victorian concoction. In 1928 a history of Fortingall was published by a local shoemaker Alexander Stewart, based on the research of one Dr A.C. Cameron, schoolmaster of Fettercairn. The story of Pontius Pilate and Fortingall was not extant before the 1870s when Cameron was doing his 'research', and the 1870s give a further key.

The 1870s saw an upsurge in church-building and interest in religious matters, so did Cameron see the possibility of linking Fortingall with the great events of the Bible Lands? According to an uncertain fourth-century tradition, Pilate killed himself on the orders of Emperor Gaius Caligula in AD 39. If this were true this was some four decades before the Roman army tramped into Perthshire, but Scottish folktale has never let reality come between it and a good story.

Foula, Shetland   TROWS

The *trows* of Shetland were the *trolls* of Norse legend; yet where the trolls were giants the trows were less than mortal size. These supernatural creatures were thought to favour the solitary island of Foula – where they spoke Norse until the 1800s – some thirty miles west of Scalloway.

Folklorists still look for the Hole of Liorafjeld on Hamna-fjeld Hill where the trows hid. The 1,000-foot hole was sealed many decades ago by a Foula man who feared the trows' powers. Visitors to Foula, folk said, risked instant death should they try to look down the hole to see the trows. In the 1600s two Dutch sailors scorned the reality of trows and were lowered into the hole. One was winched out dead and the other died en route to his vessel.

Fowlis Wester, Tayside OSSIAN

Six miles north-east of Crieff, Fowlis Wester is known for its ancient, 10-foot Celtic Cross, enriched with Pictish symbols, figures and ancient sculpture. Until the eighteenth century it was known as the Lark's Stone and thereafter as *Clach Ossian,* marking the grave of the legendary warrior-bard Ossian. When the stone was moved to widen the road in the 1730s an urn burial was found and a reburial was made straight away to avoid bad luck from the exhumation. William Wordsworth (1770–1850) made it the subject of a poem with the lines: 'In this still place, remote from men/ Sleeps Ossian ...'

G

Gavinton, Berwickshire, Borders FAIRIES

Sir Alexander James Edmund Cockburn (1802–80) of Langton, a hamlet some two miles south-west of Duns, was the last of his line. On the death of this prominent lawyer a curious tale circulated concerning earth tremors that had occurred in the previous century, and how folklore connected them with a previous Cockburn baronet and the fairies.

Folktale had it that the fairies of nearby Duns Law were in dispute with the Cockburns concerning lands around the Langton Burn, and that these supernatural creatures threatened to move the Cockburn mansion to Dogden Moss over the moors near Greenlaw. One night the fairies began to loosen the foundations of the house (earth tremors in reality) and the activities woke the family. Laird Cockburn heaved up the sash of one of the front windows and cried out: 'Lord keep us and the house together,' whereupon, the folktale continued, the potency of his impassioned prayer broke the fairies' power and the house sank back to a safe rest. The mansion was demolished in the 1920s.

Glamis, Angus   FAIRIES/WITCH/GHOSTS

Because of its long associations with Scottish royal and political history, Glamis Castle has a prime position in the country's folklore. Even its beginnings were placed in fairy-lore.

Undoubtedly there had been a fortified building of sorts on this site some time before Sir John Lyon of Forteviot was made Thane of Glamis in 1372 by his soon-to-be father-in-law King Robert II. Around the time of his marriage to the Princess Joanna, Sir John began to reconstruct the fortification at Glamis, and the superstitious wondered if the building work would be disrupted as it had before.

Folkloric tradition has it that the building of Glamis Castle was started on nearby Hunter's Hill – which many were to point out as the site of the assassination of King Malcolm II in 1034. The place had been called 'The Fiery Pans' after the site of the beacon fires once lit there by the primitive tribesmen who lived in the surrounding hills. Here, too, the superstitious said, dwelt the fairy folk whose whims had to be humoured or disaster fall. As the castle began to be constructed in its first form, the fairy folk knocked down by night the stones built up by day, until the builders received a direction from an unseen voice which echoed round the hills saying: 'Building the castle in a bog, where 'twill neither shak not shog.' Thus folklore explains how Glamis Castle came to be built in the flat low-lying Vale of Strathmore.

The Bowes-Lyons of Glamis dotted in and out of history as courtiers and soldiers. One lady was to suffer terribly for her association with the family. Because of James V's vendetta against the Douglas family, Janet Douglas, widow of the 6th Lord Glamis, was falsely accused of sorcery and was burned as a witch on Castle Hill, Edinburgh on 14 July 1537.

Glamis began to be associated with the myths surrounding the Scottish cult hero Macbeth through Shakespeare's play. In *Macbeth* Shakespeare wrote:

This castle hath a pleasant seat; the air
Nimbly and sweetly recommends itself
Unto our gentle senses.

The many references to Glamis in the tragedy have led to speculation that the play was actually set in the Glamis of the time. Some folklorists even claim that Shakespeare passed near Glamis and glimpsed Macbeth's Castle of Dunsinane, Birnham Wood and Duncan's Camp, when his friend Lawrence Fletcher brought the bard and a group of players to Aberdeen in 1599 to entertain King James VI. Today such theories are encouraged by the naming of two rooms 'King Malcolm's Room' and 'Duncan's Hall' in the castle guidebook, even though, for instance Duncan MacCrinan, High King of Scotland, was dead for three centuries before this particular 'Hall' was constructed.

Great interest in Glamis was engendered in 1923 when Prince Albert, Duke of York, the second son of King George V married Lady Elizabeth Bowes-Lyon, the younger daughter of the 14th Earl and Countess of Strathmore and Kinghorne. Thereafter royal biographies began to mention Glamis folklore and list its ghosts from the 'Grey Lady', who is said to materialise in the chapel, to the ghostly negro boy who waits patiently on a seat in the 'Queen Mother's Sitting Room'.

Yet, the folktales of Glamis are most concerned with the supposed 'secret room' – talked about since Sir Walter Scott's time when he visited Glamis in 1791 – and the 'Monster of Glamis'. The first is probably based on fact, the second the family usually denies hotly.

Because of the thickness of the walls – some running to 15 feet – there are several tales of secret rooms carved out of these depths. One is said to lead off 'The Crypt' and in true romantic style is dressed up in legend. It is said that in this room one of the Lords of Glamis and the Earl of Crawford played cards with the Devil himself on the Sabbath. So great were the resulting disturbances that eventually the room was permanently sealed. In his *Book of Record,* under the date 1684, Patrick, 3rd Earl of Strathmore, makes mention of 'closet' being constructed in the thickness of the walls.

Even the most 'authentic' of biographies concerning Queen Elizabeth, the Queen Mother, mention Glamis's 'monster'. One biographer, Michael Thornton, in 1985 even identified the characters in the legend. He averred that Charlotte, wife of Thomas, Lord Glamis, heir to the 11th Earl, gave birth to a hideously deformed child who could never inherit the title. This was in 1821, so this 'monster' was locked away in Glamis to live to a very old age. It is even said that a workman who inadvertently discovered the secret – which was held only by succeeding earls of Strathmore – was 'paid off'. Despite many denials the story persists.

Primitive inhabitants of Scotland knew of the healing power of touch, a part of their knowledge of mystic psychosomatic magic. They leave us clues of this in their cave-drawings of human hands as separate objects. At first it is likely that this healing power was practised by tribal shamans only, but in time the power was also invested in chiefs and sovereigns.

One disease which is often referred to in historical documents (like those of Glamis) as being healed by touch is scrofula (tuberculosis of the lymphatic glands, with suppurating abscesses and fistulous passages), known also as the 'King's Evil'. There grew up an associated healing ceremony known a 'Touching for the King's Evil'. It became a part of English court ritual by the twelfth century. Scots-born kings who continued the ritual were James VI & I and his son Charles I, and James VII & II held touching ceremonies too. During his visit to Glamis Castle in 1716, the latter king's son, Prince James Francis Edward Stuart, the 'Old Pretender' and Jacobite King James VIII & III, touched for the King's Evil in the chapel at Glamis Castle. On this occasion he distributed special 'touch pieces'; these were coin/medals marked with the putative king's name and the inscription *Soli Deo Gloria* ('Glory to God Alone'), and in themselves they became amulets to prevent a variety of illnesses.

Glenelg, Inverness, Highland   OSSIAN/SNAKE CULT

Glenelg is not only famous for its views over the Sound of

Sleat in Skye, but in folklore it was the hunting-ground of the third-century Celtic hero, Fionn, son of Camulos, a king of the Tuatha de Danann (the Children of Don). Fionn's fairy woman gave birth on Arisaig to his son, the warrior-bard Ossian, whose childhood was said to have been spent at Glenelg.

James Macpherson (1736–96), the poet, produced various 'Ossianic fragments' which he averred were Ossian's own writings during 1762–63, under the titles *Fingal* and *Temora*. The compositions were an assembly of Gaelic myths which Macpherson interlarded with his own genre writings, yet without Macpherson the Gaelic myths and folkloric trends might have been lost.

At Glenelg, too, there is the ancient mound by Sealasaig Farm, associated with a primitive serpent cult. The site was sacred to the Celtic fire goddess, Bride, daughter of Dagda, King of the Tuatha de Danann and Baonn, Queen of Ireland. In the Christian ascendancy Bride became St Brigid, patroness of the poor. On her feast day, 1 February, it was said that the 'serpent saint' appears on the mound.

At Glenelg, too, folklorists point out John MacInnes's Loch. Here a local crofter of that name was drowned in the 1890s; he was said to have been lured into the peaty waters by a kelpie.

Gordonstoun, Morayshire, Grampian   WARLOCK

Another larger-than-life character who folklore invested with supernatural powers was the 'warlock' Sir Robert Gordon (1647–1704). The records of 1678 show how Sir Robert managed to extend his life span by giving his shadow to the Devil. In the north-east areas of Scotland it is believed that an individual's shadow is a part of the soul, and everyone knew that those who could work magic – which Sir Robert had learned while studying at Padua – cast no shadow. Having no more important gifts to give the Devil, Sir Robert built for himself the Devil-proof fortress at Gordonstoun known as the Round Square Tower, constructed as a mystic circle. There he took refuge with a minister for company. At length the minister persuaded Sir Robert that he would be much safer from the Devil's machinations if he sought sanctuary at Birnie Church, a handful of miles south of nearby Elgin. Sir Robert was so persuaded, but the old tale recounted how the Devil waylaid the knight and his clerical companion. This is how locals explained Sir Robert's death in 1704 and there were those ready to attest that they had seen the Devil assault Sir Robert, put him over the saddle of his demonic horse and gallop off to the 'Fires of Hell' with a large 'demon dog running beside them with its fangs buried deep' in Sir Robert's neck. The minister later met a mysterious end too.

Today Sir Robert's seventeenth-century Round Square Tower is a part of Gordonstoun School, founded in 1934 by Kurt Hahn.

The nearest large town to Gordonstoun is Elgin which had regular witch-hunts for a hundred years from 1560. The last witch trial at Elgin was in 1662 when Margaret Kellie and Barbara Innes were found guilty of witchcraft and executed on 11 May.

H

Hawick, Roxburghshire, Borders   KELPIE

Once the centre of Scotland's woollens, yarns and hosiery industry, Hawick is still nationally famous for its 'Riding of the Marches' at the beginning of June. Its folklore, too, has added a few tales to the nation's supernatural history.

A particular tale concerns the kelpie which dwelt by the source of Slitrig Water on the Winchburgh Hill, on the northern side of the Liddesdale Watershed. The Kelpie was always irritated if anyone threw a stone into the water by its dwelling-place. For someone to do so resulted in the Kelpie releasing a large amount of water to flood the valley below. Folklore says that this is how Hawick came to be inundated in the eighteenth century, for, by accident, a shepherd rolled a large stone into the Kelpie's loch. The folklorist John Leyden collected this doggerel about the event:

Nor long the time, if village-saws be true,
Since in the deep a hardy peasant threw
A pondrous stone; when murmuring from below,
With gushing sound he heard the loch o'erflow.

The mighty torrent, foaming down the hills,
Called, with strong voice, on all her subject rills;
Rocks drove on jagged rocks with thundering sound,
And the red waves, impatient, rent their mound.

On Hawick burst the flood's resistless sway,
Ploughed the paved streets, and tore the walls away,
Floated high roofs, from whelming fabrics torn;
While pillared arches down the wave were borne.

Hopekirk, Roxburghshire, Borders   GHOST

In a secluded part of Hopekirk churchyard is to be found the following inscription:

Here lys Nicol Edgar, son of the Laird of Wedderlie, who died the 31st May, 1724, aged 67 years. And his spouse Susanna, who died 30th June, 1713, aged 52.

Although the little church at Hopekirk, some seven miles south-east of Hawick, dates from 1858, its site marks the foundations of an earlier building. In 1694, the Rev. Nicol Edgar moved to the parish of Hopekirk (then known as Hobkirk) to minister a rather superstitious community. For a long time the kirk had been considered an encumbrance and had fallen into bad repair, with its unsafe roof threatening the congregation every Sunday. In the end, the fear of entombment became so strong that the elders started a subscription list for the new kirk. In 1690 work started on a new building of barn-like shape, with low roof, clay floor and thatched heather roof. Little better than its predecessor, the church was finished in 1692. In this church ministered the Rev. Nicol Edgar.

For thirty years the Rev. Edgar tended to the spiritual needs of the parish and wrestled with many a problem on their behalf. His greatest perplexity, however, was not of human nature. Exactly when the mysterious happenings first occurred, no one can tell, but many who passed the church-yard at dusk often saw the tall man with a blue bonnet prowling among the tombs. Children at play were frightened by the man's sudden appearance and the grave-digger refused to do any more work, for the man watched him continually as he dug.

The patience of the elders came to an end on the day the ghostly man appeared at a church service scaring all the nervous into fainting fits. The minister, the elders declared, would have to do something about the apparition.

Armed with his big kirk bible and a rusty claymore, the Rev. Edgar set out one evening to investigate the mystery. As he passed through the graveyard all was quiet, not a blade of grass rustled in the chill evening air, nor did any spectre appear from behind a stone. Silence reigned too, in the kirk. Only the minister disturbed the peace, his keys rattling loudly in the lock as the door creaked open. Quickly walking across the empty church, the Rev. Edgar mounted the pulpit, laid the bible on the rest, put his claymore near to hand, said a prayer, and awaited developments.

As the hour of midnight approached an owl hooted outside, waking the minister from the light slumber which had overtaken him. Then, gradually, the dark church was lit by a pale blue light.

In a few moments even the darkest niche of the church was brightly illuminated. To the minister's complete amaze-ment the figure of a man with knee-breeches, brown coat, blue bonnet and stockings appeared at the east end of the church.

Edgar immediately recognised the man as the one who had terrorised his parishioners with sudden appearances. Walking steadily forward, the apparition turned and faced the cleric. The minister gripped his sword as the stranger looked him up and down. Plucking up courage the minister asked the stranger why he frightened the parish.

A short time past, explained the apparition, he had been a cattle-dealer. One day on the moors, as he walked home from Hawick Lammas Fair, he had been murdered. His spirit could never rest until the murderers had been found and punished. He begged the minister, with the promise that he would harm no one, to allow him a piece of ground in the parish where his restless spirit might walk to and fro without hindrance until his murderers were found.

'Puir body,' said the minister. 'I'll no' grudge ye that. Henceforth, until the Lord gives you wearifu' speerit rest, ye shall trouble Hobkirk no more, but shall walk in a straight line atween Hoddleswoodie and Howabank, on the lands of the Hoppisburn.' From that day the apparition was never seen in Hopekirk churchyard again.

The Rev. Edgar was never the same after his experience with the ghost, neither was he the same in the minds of his parishioners. Fear of the blue-bonneted man turned into fear of the minister. Any many who could talk to a ghost, reasoned the good folk of Hopekirk, must have something of the Devil in him as well. Four years after his night vigil the minister died, but the fear of him still lived in the surrounding hamlets. Perhaps the minister's ghost would walk now, gossiped the parishioners.

One night in early June 1724, a party of young bloods broke into the minister's tomb and hauled his body away across the moors towards Bonchester Hill. As the carriers roughly manhandled the corpse, one of the arms got loose from the rope which bound them and the chill dead hand of the minister slapped one of the desecrators across the face. Terror-struck the young men dropped their burden and ran away.

All night and for most part of the next day the dead minister lay on the moor. Finally he was found and replaced in his tomb. From that day no one dared even cut the grass around the grave of the remarkable minister of Hopekirk who could reason with ghosts lest they disturb his spirit to retribution.

Those who constantly work with animals develop a certain rapport with them, and Scottish folklore is full of examples of humankind and animal kind sharing adventures. Most mentioned in such connections were the grooms, blacksmiths and carters who were said to be privy to the secret charm known as the Horseman's Word. With such a charm even the most savage stallions could be tamed and galloping horses arrested in mid-flight.

In Scotland those whose daily life involved horses were presumed to be bonded together in a society known as the Brotherhood of the Horseman's Word. The secrets of the charm were learned at Brotherhood meetings, and a centre of the folklore of the cult was at Huntly where the Bogie and the Deveron meet in confluence.

Local folklore records show that initiations to the Brotherhood usually took place at Martinmas (11 November) in a farmyard setting, a barn or an out-house. Usually, too, a band of thirteen (or any odd number) of initiates went through a secret ceremony of masonic-like ritual. Once initiated the novices would be given the necessary secrets in handling horses.

Folklorists believe that in some areas the Horseman's Word was linked with a local witch-cult, and certainly the Devil was invoked in some rituals, or 'the first horseman', the biblical Cain, as mentioned in the Horseman's Toast:

> *Here's to the horse with the four white feet,*
> *The chestnut tail and mane –*
> *A star on his face and a spot on his breast,*
> *And his master's name was Cain.*

Some folklorists have suggested that the secret of the charm lay in voice modulation, sound vibration and skill in horse management. Thus the early horsemen of the primitive tribes of Scotland passed down their skills right up to the days when horse-power began to diminish.

I

Innerleithen, Borders

Traquair is dubbed 'the oldest inhabited house in Scotland' and is set in Peebleshire, six miles from Peebles. It is a house rich in Jacobite and Catholic folklore, from the relics of Mary, Queen of Scots, and Bonnie Prince Charlie to the priests' secret staircase. Its late laird, Peter Maxwell Stuart, though, emphasised 'the House has no ghosts'. A folk memory of the Stuarts is encountered at the main approach of the house in the Bear Gates of Traquair. Tradition has it that the last person to pass through these gates was Charles Edward Stuart, and that Charles Stuart (1697–1764), the 5th Earl of Traquair, vowed that they would remain closed until a Stuart restoration to the throne was effected. As poet William Henry Ogilvie (1869–1963) put it:

> *The wind through the rusted iron sings,*
> *The sun on the self-sown tangle burns,*
> *But never a hoof on the roadway rings –*
> *The gate is shut till the King returns.*

To add to the folklore story, however, writing in 1927 the topographer L. Russell Muirhead noted that the gates 'have never been opened since they were closed in 1796 on the death of the 7th (and, as it proved, last) Countess of Traquair [Mary Stuart, wife of the 7th Earl] 'until an eighth countess should enter'.

Today Innerleithen is known for St Ronan's Well. By the 1780s Innerleithen was no more than a small hamlet of thatched biggins at the base of Lee Pen. On its slopes, however, were ancient springs and the Doo Well, so called because of the large number of wood pigeons in its vicinity. For decades the waters of the well had been drunk and anointed as a cure for eye disorders and skin complaints. In 1824 Sir Walter Scott used the Well as the background for his novel *St Ronan's Well* and the whole area was popularised. St Ronan, by the by, was an early Celtic bishop, well-known from Brittany to Scotland.

At the time of the novel's publication, Innerleithen was within the estate of Charles Stuart (1781–1861), 8th (and last) Earl of Traquair, and he promoted the Well as a tourist attraction. He was the founder of the St Ronan's Club, whose current members organise the St Ronan's Border Games. Here, too, takes place the 'Cleikum Ceremony', which was introduced in 1901 to teach Innerleithen's young folk about the legend of St Ronan, who is traditionally depicted attacking Satan with his pastoral crook. St Ronan hooks ('cleiks' in Border parlance) the Devil by his nose and Christianity triumphs. In 1990 an Interpretive Centre was opened to promote the folklore of Innerleithen and its customs.

Inverary, Argyllshire, Strathclyde   GHOSTLY MUSIC

Inverary Castle, home of the Dukes of Argyll, is haunted by the 'Harper of Inverary'. Heard in the area of the Blue Room the ghost is thought to be that of a man hanged at the time the Marquis of Montrose was hunting down the then laird.

Invergarry, Inverness,   FAMILY FOLKLORE/WELL
Highland

Invergarry, by Loch Oich, has a strange memorial by the road as visitors journey south. It is known as *Tobar nan Ceann* ('Well of the Heads'). In 1663 one Alasdair MacDonell was plotting a bid for the chieftainship of the MacDonells of Keppoch and Garragach, and murdered Alexander, 12th chief of Keppoch and his brother. By 1665 Alasdair and his six accomplices were arrested and beheaded; theirs are the seven heads of the well's monument. Folklore has it that as the arresting posse took the severed heads of the miscreants to Inverness there was much tumult in the carrying sack, with the heads gnashing teeth and groaning. To silence them the captain of the posse washed them in Loch Ness.

I mo Chridhe, I mo Ghraidh ('Iona my heart, Iona my love') said St Columba, and Iona remained long an emotive name in the lore of the Picts, Scots and the Norsemen. It was also a part of the legends of the prominent monasteries of Northumbria, for Northumbrian kings and clerics were brought into the Celtic fringe through the teachings of the Iona community.

The island of Iona, less than a mile from its neighbour of Mull, enters Scotland's story when St Columba arrived from Ireland in 563 to bring Christianity to the mainland of Scotland. The Columban community was succeeded by the Benedictine and Augustinian communities, and in 1266 Norway ceded the islands to the Scottish Crown.

Iona was rich in the folklore of a wider spectrum than just that of the Norse sagas, for the Columban Church was the cultural force of the first united kingdom of the Picts and Scots under Kenneth mac Alpin (r.843–58), and he is said to lie amongst the royal bones with the folk cult-heroes Duncan and Macbeth at the graveyard *Reilig Odhrain*. Not for nothing did the princelings of the Celtic north-west want to be buried at Iona, for the blessing of the soil was said to expunge all sin.

Scottish folklore invests Iona with ghostly monks, fairy music, phantom lights, spectral Viking longboats, and evil elements kept at bay by the 'call' of St Columba whose island would be all that would be saved at the biblical Apocalypse, the old tales recounted. Even its stones were sources of authority; to the Black Stones came generations of Highland chieftains to swear their allegiances. The Druid Stone too was said to help fishermen navigate the treacherous waters hereabouts. Now two thousand years of folklore shares a presence with the Iona Community founded in 1938, the Iona Cathedral Trust established by the then Duke of Argyll in 1899, and the National Trust for Scotland who acquired most of the rest of Iona in 1978.

The royal burgh where Robert Burns came to learn flax-dressing during 1781–83, Irvine is particularly remembered in Scottish folklore because of its August Marymass Fair.

The fair dates from the twelfth century, but the accompanying races are deemed much older. In medieval times it was the fair of the Blessed Virgin Mary, but later was associated with Mary, Queen of Scots. It was once organised by the Carters' Society. A central figure of the fair is the Marymass Queen, usually dressed these days as a mock Mary, Queen of Scots.

J

Jedburgh, Roxburghshire, Borders   GHOST/CUSTOM

Once the county town of Roxburgh, the royal burgh of Jedburgh is famous in history for its castle, whose site developed as the local prison, the Augustinian abbey and the burgh's 'Jeddart Justice', wherein a supposed miscreant was executed first and then tried. Yet, it is to the records of the twelfth-century abbey that folklore looks for its most celebrated story.

During October 1285 the abbey witnessed the marriage of King Alexander III and the Frenchwoman Yolande, daughter of the Comte de Dreux, by Abbot John Morel. A grand banquet was held following the religious ceremony and at it a masque was enacted, written specially, it is said, by Thomas the Rhymer. As actors and actresses capered in the masque, to the horror of all, a spectral skeleton wrapped in a shroud threaded its way through the dancers to disappear as quietly as it had appeared. Before the wraith left, however, it pointed a beckoning finger at the king and his new bride. The company took the event as an evil omen.

On 19 March 1286, Thomas the Rhymer prophesied to the Earl of March at Dunbar that before midnight 'a blast so vehement that it shall exceed all those that have yet been heard in Scotland' would occur. Most folk expected a storm to follow, but all were struck to sorrow when a messenger came to Dunbar with news that King Alexander had fallen over the cliffs at Pettycur Bay, Fife, during the storm as he made his way to Yolande and the court at Kinghorn Castle.

Thus the evil omen of the spectral skeleton was felt in Scotland, and there was to be worse. Alexander's heir, his eight-year-old granddaughter Margaret, Maid of Norway, drowned on her way to her coronation in Scotland in 1290, and Scotland was plunged into acrimonious jockeying for the crown.

Jedburgh is also celebrated in folklore for its Ba' Game. Two games were well established on Candlemas Day (2 February – the Boys' Ba' Game) and at Fastern E'en (Shrove Tuesday – Mens' Ba' Game). In both two teams, the Uppies (those born above the line of the old Mercat Cross) and the Doonies (those born below the Mercat Cross) competed with a ball to which coloured streamers were attached. The game is played through the streets and often into the River Jed. Today the Jethart Callants' Festival takes place in early July. Concerning the folklore origins of the game: one school of thought averts that it began as a memory of a battle between locals and an invading English army, the ribboned ball representing an oozing severed English head.

John O'Groats, Caithness LEGENDS

Despite not being the actual northernmost point of Scotland – the sandstone promontory of Dunnet Head in the Pentland Firth is that – John O'Groats was long the traditional end or starting point in the 876-metre races to and from Land's End. Legend has it that it was named after Dutchman Joannes de Groote, who came to Scotland sometime in the sixteenth century.

It is said that to avoid quarrels between the eight beneficiaries of his will, de Groote built an octagonal house, with eight doors and an octagonal table. Thus each could enter by a personal door and sit at the 'head' of the table.

K

Kemnay, Grampian WITCHLORE

Once the stone was hewn from Kemnay quarries for the piers of the Forth Railway Bridge, but folklore indicates a different stone, for here at the Long Stone o' Craigearn the Aberdeenshire witches convened in defiance of the bishops of Aberdeen whose seat was at nearby Fetternear House.

Kilconquhar, Fife WITCHLORE

Pronounced 'kinnuchar', and once the cell of St Conacher, Kilconquhar was the execution place for witches of the East Neuk of Fife. Here in its loch the Devil's beldames perished by drowning. As late as 1705 Pittenweem clergy pursued witches and of Kilconquhar's witch associations one balladist wrote:

> *They tied her arms behind her back*
> *And twisted them wi' a pin,*
> *And they dragged her to Kilconquhar Loch,*
> *An' coupit the limmer in.*   threw in the villain/whore

Kildrummy, Grampian CULT HERO

Near this Aberdeenshire village is the cult hero stone of Lulach. Gruoch, wife of Gillecomgain, Mormaer of Moray, and granddaughter of King Kenneth III, later became wife to Macbeth, who adopted her son Lulach.

Lulach was crowned *Ard Righ na h-Alba* (High King of Scotland) at Scone in 1057. A year later he was slain, say the chroniclers, at Essie, Strathbogie. This stone became a symbol of his spirit and was so venerated.

Killiecrankie, Tayside FOLK HEROES

Some three miles north of Pitlochry the Pass of Killiecrankie has been gouged by the River Garry as it plunges its way to join the Tummel by Faskally. Historically it is known for the Battle of Killiecrankie of 27 July 1689 when the Jacobite John Graham of Claverhouse, Viscount Dundee (*c.*1649–89), vanquished the loyalist army of General Hugh Mackay, in the name of King James VII & II. John Graham was himself mortally wounded in the opening volleys of the battle; he was buried in the Old Church of Blair.

Undoubtedly the best-known story within the folklore of the battle is that associated with Soldier's Leap. The soldier mentioned was Donald MacBean and he left this memoir in 1728:

> *The sun going down caused the Highlandmen to advance on us like madmen, without shoe or stocking, covering themselves from our fire with their targes; at last they cast away their musquets, drew their broadswords, and advanced furiously upon us, and were in the middle of us before we could fire three shots apiece, broke us, and obliged us to retreat.*
>
> *Some fled to the water and some another way (we were for the most part new men) I fled to the baggage, and took a horse in order to ride the water; there follows me a Highlandman with sword and targe, in order to take the horse and kill myself … I kept always the horse betwixt him and me; at length he drew his pistol, and I fled; he fired after me. I went above the Pass, where I met with another water very deep; it was about 18 foot over between two rocks. I resolved to jump it, so I laid down my gun and hat and jumped, and lost one of my shoes in the jump. Many of our men were lost in that water.*

A visitor centre, operated by the National Trust for Scotland, celebrates the history and famous events associated with Killiecrankie.

Killin, Tayside   FOLK HERO

Housed within St Fillans Mill, by the Falls of Dochart, are relics of a real-life folk hero. Near the site of the reconstructed mill would sit Fillan, the Irish prince-cum-Celtic missionary who came to Scotland in the eighth century with his mother St Kentigerna and his kinsman the abbot St Comgan. St Fillan was to be one of the most renowned of the Scoto-Irish saints, and King Robert I, the Bruce, venerated the relics – a jewelled arm-bone – of St Fillan before the Battle of Bannock-burn in 1314, and encouraged Abbot Maurice of Inchaffray to exhort the saint for victory for the Scottish army before the conflict. So highly did Robert rate St Fillan's powers that he gave grants of lands at Killin and Strathfillan to the Perthshire Augustinian abbey of Inchaffray in Strathearn to increase their economic dignity and carry out their work in the name of the saint.

In this mountain territory called Breadalbane, around Killin, where Celtic lore, fairies and kelpies are still talked about, St Fillan spread the Gospel and at the mill are preser-ved the Healing Stones which St Fillan blessed. The stones were used for curing illnesses and healing ailments until the nineteenth century, and the layer of river wrack (straw, twigs and so on) on which the stones rest is changed every Christ-mas Eve. Although St Fillan was venerated on his feast day of 9 January in the Scottish medieval calendar, the 20 January is now observed in Killin as St Fillan's Day.

Kirk Yetholm, Roxburghshire, Borders

GYPSYLORE

Yetholm is made up of the two villages of Kirk Yetholm and Town Yetholm. Divided by the Bowmont Water they are still associated in Scottish folk history as being the home of the 'Scottish Gypsy Kings'. The first mention of gypsies in Scotland is in the accounts of the Lord High Treasurer of 1505, in which King James IV disbursed at Stirling a sum of money in favour of the gypsies. It is likely that gypsies (often referred to at this time as 'Egyptians', although they originated in north-west India) were known in Scotland before this date as an identifiable group, for they were hailed as 'great healers' in old chronicles, and it is said that King James V was cured by a gypsy folk-healer while he was in France. The Faa family were the most prominent gypsies in Scotland's folk history and in 1537 one Paul Faa's name is recorded on a charge of murder. An Order in Court of 1541 was taken out against gypsies and thereafter they were mostly confined to the debatable lands around the Scottish Border from where they could flee to England if the law came too close for comfort.

The first Scottish Gypsy King about whom anything is positively known was Wull Faa (c. 1700–84). One of the most colourful gypsy 'rulers' was Esther Faa Blyth (d.1883) who lived at 'The Palace', a building which still exists at Yetholm. The last coronation of a Scottish Gypsy King took place in 1898 when Esther's son Charles Blyth Faa II (1825–1902) was crowned. Today there are still descendants in the area. The 'Gypsy Kingdom' was never recognised in law, but several gypsies were given places to live by the Bennets of Grubet, who owned Kirk Yetholm in antiquity, so that the twin villages became the 'Kingdom'.

Kirk Yetholm was the scene, too, of a scheme aimed at encouraging the gypsies to settle down. It was organised by the Rev. John Baird and the Edinburgh-based Society for the Reformation of the Gypsies. Gypsy children were cared for while their parents were away hawking, and a school for them met with some success. Many gypsy men were competent violinists and pipers (Jamie Baillie – d.1861 – was the most famous Border gypsy violinist) and the gypsies had their own language and lore.

Kirkcaldy, Fife   WIZARD

The ancient, but now ruined, Tower of Balwearie in the old parish of Abbotshall, was the purported birthplace and main residence of Michael Scot (c. 1175–c. 1234), known as 'The Wizard'. Here at the tower, some one-and-a-half miles west of modern Kirkcaldy, Scot was deemed to have hatched his devious plots that folklore said were to cleave the Eildon Hills to be split into their recognisable shapes, and to cause the plague to be locked up in a vault at Luce Abbey.

Scot – whose background is factually obscure – was given a wider audience by being portrayed with some power in

Canto II of Sir Walter Scott's *The Lay of the Last Minstrel* (1805):

> *In these far climes it was my lot*
> *To meet the wondrous Michael Scot;*
> *A wizard of such dreadful fame,*
> *That when, in Salamanca's cave,*
> *Him listed his magic wand to wave,*
> *The bells would ring in Notre Dame!*
> *Some of his skills he taught to me;*
> *And, Warrior, I could say to thee*
> *The words that cleft Eildon Hills in three.*
> *And bridled the Tweed with a curb of stone:*
> *But to speak them were a deadly sin ...*

Yet Scot was probably a scholar of some great merit before Scott's verses, even though the biographies of three Michael Scots of Balwearie during *c.* 1175–1290 may have been run together to make a whole. He is said by such historians as Patrick Fraser Tytler (1791–1849) to have studied at Oxford, was a courtier of Emperor Frederick II and is said to have learned magic at Padua. Indeed folktales about his demon horse, and demon ship are given prominence in such works as Dante's *Inferno* (Canto XX), and his volumes on alchemy are well known.

Here is a typical folktale about Michael Scot based on medieval interpretation: On one occasion the King of Scots was angry at the attacks by French pirates on Scottish vessels at sea, so he commanded Michael Scot to go to France as ambassador to petition the king to have the outrages stopped. Scot opened his magic *Book of Might* and read out a spell to conjure up his black demon horse. Mounting the mare, Scot sped through the air to France.

Haughtily striding into the French king's presence Scot relayed the wishes of his Scottish master. The King of France demurred and made to wave Scot from his presence. Scot whistled up his demonic horse and commanded it to stamp its hooves three times. On the first stamp all the bells of the churches of Paris were set jangling. On the second three towers of the palace collapsed, and as the horse made to stamp a third time ... the king capitulated. Orders were given to the French seamen to end their piracy and Scot left to recount the good news to his king.

Sir Walter Scott delighted in taking groups of visitors to his home at Abbotsford on expeditions to Melrose Abbey. Solemnly he would point out the supposed site of Michael Scot's tomb in the south transept with the added folklore that somewhere beneath their feet lay Scot's magic tome the *Book of Might*.

Kirkpatrick-Fleming, Dumfries & Galloway
CULT/FOLK HERO

The folklore of Robert I, the Bruce, erstwhile Earl of Carrick, born at Turnberry Castle, Ayrshire, in 1274, is perhaps the best known in Scotland. His story of struggle to free his country, from 1297 until his great defeat of the English at Bannockburn in 1314, has been oft retold. His folklore stretch-ed throughout the four corners of Scotland – from Tain, Highland – where his second wife Elizabeth de Burgh and daughter Marjory sought refuge at the Firth (sanctuary) of St Duthac against the pro-English Earl of Ross – to Whithorn, Dumfries & Galloway – where he knelt in prayer at the Shrine of St Ninian; and from Dunaverty Castle, Strathclyde captured by Bruce – to Auldcambus, Borders – where legend has it he built wooden siege engines in the now vanished forest.

Yet it is to Kirkpatrick-Fleming, not far from Gretna Green, that folklorists look for perhaps the most famous folklore of all about Bruce – his encounter with the didactic spider. Local legend has it that Bruce Cave hereabouts is the one in which Bruce's resolve was strengthened by a spider's tenacity. Here's a mid-Victorian version of the legend from James Taylor's *The Pictorial History of Scotland*:

> *The king was lying one morning upon a handful of straw, and deliberating whether he ought not to abandon all further attempts to make good his right to the Scottish*

crown, and transporting himself to the Holy Land, spending the remainder of his life fighting against the Saracens. It happened, that while he was thus pondering, he looked upward to the roof of the hut in which he lay, and his eye was attracted by the exertions of a spider, who, in order to fix its web, was endeavouring to swing itself from one crevice to another above his head. Involuntarily he became interested in the pertinacity with which the insect renewed his exertions. At length, after it had tried to carry its point six times, but without success, it occurred to him that he had himself fought just six battles against the enemies of his country, and he resolved that he would decide his own course according to the success or failure of the spider. At the seventh effort, the insect gained its object, and Bruce in like manner persevered, and never afterwards met with any decisive check or defeat in his efforts to vindicate his own rights and the freedom of Scotland. Hence it has been held unlucky or ungraceful, or both, in one of the name of Bruce to kill a spider.

In reality at the time usually associated with the story, September 1306, Bruce had fled from Dunaverty Castle to Rathlin Island, Co. Antrim; but yet again folklore has never altered reality to spoil a good story.

Bruce died in 1329 at his house at Cardross. His body with the heart removed was buried at Dunfermline Abbey; yet the heart took on a new folklore of its own. It was taken by James, Lord of Douglas, to Spain to be carried in the fight against the Moors. Eventually the heart was returned and buried near the high altar of Melrose Abbey.

Knocklearoch, Killarow and Kilmeny, Islay   SANCTUARY

The medieval concept of sanctuary, wherein a miscreant escaping the law, or anyone being pursued by enemies of whatever kind, could enter the precincts of a church, priory or abbey and remain there in freedom from arrest or capture for a certain length of time, was widely accepted in Scotland.

Folklore, however, gave sanctuary a longer history.

At Killarow and Kilmeny are to be found the Knock-learoch Standing Stones. Although playing some role in a long-forgotten ritual, folktale recounts they were two former priests who were hanged on the site and petrified by supernatural hands. Local legend has it that there were once three stones arranged in a triangle and within their inner area anyone who needed it could seek sanctuary.

Kyleakin, Skye   FOLK HEROINE

On the promontory of Kyleakin, at the head of Loch Alsh, and across from Kyle of Lochalsh, stands Castle Moil. Folklore has it that the castle was built at the order of a Viking princess who married one of the Macdonalds, Lords of the Isles. This lady was very jealous of her properties and is said to have had a huge chain stretched across the Kyle to help levy a toll from vessels plying between Loch Alsh and the Inner Sound. Folklore gave her the curious name of 'Saucy Mary'.

L

Lamberton, Berwickshire, Borders   WITCHLORE

After 1754 Gretna Green became the mecca for thwarted English lovers defying the marriage laws of the day, yet in the history of romantic irregular marriages Lamberton Toll also had its trade in eloping lovers and a whole line of blacksmiths plied their unusual nuptial rites at the Border crossing.

Three miles north of Berwick-on-Tweed, where the emissaries of King James IV met Margaret Tudor, daughter of Henry VIII of England in 1502, to convey her to her Scottish wedding, lies the ruined church of Lamberton and a little to the west on Mordington Hill was conducted altogether different trade. Here on Witches' Knowe supposed practitioners of the black arts were executed up to 1700.

The old medieval town of Lanark which down the years has laid claim to be the home (in Castlegate) and the marriage place (in the twelfth-century church of St Kentigern) of the patriot William Wallace, adds some important facets to the history of folklore in Scotland.

'Lanark Lanimers' – from the old Scots word meaning 'boundaries of land' – remains as a week-long festival in June to celebrate the annual inspection of the march (boundary) stones of the burgh made royal by King David I in 1140. The custom has almost nine centuries of tradition of local officials checking the boundaries and develops into a ceremonial to crown the Lanimer Queen (a custom which began in 1893).

Lanark also has the custom of 'Whuppity Scoorie', which developed into a piece of modern folklore. It appears that in the latter part of the nineteenth century they conducted 'The Wee Bell Ceremony'. After a silence of six months a small bell – which had once sounded the town curfew – was rung on 1 March to ring again at the same hour for the following six months. A group of youths would gather as the bell was tolled and as it sounded they would march down to New Lanark and engage the boys there in battle. At first it was sparring with their caps tied up with string as weapons, and later it degenerated into fisticuffs. After 1880 there was a trend towards stone throwing. On one occasion they even beat the local police who had gathered to separate the gangs:

Hurrah, boys, Hurrah. We have won the day,
We've beaten Sergeant Sutherland and chased his men away.

The name of the custom 'Whuppity Scoorie' seems to date from 1893, coining the name from that of a Scottish evil spirit of antiquity.

Langholm, Dumfries & Galloway   SUPERSTITION

On the River Esk, Langholm is associated in folklore with the Border Reivers (robbers, usually of cattle) in general, and with Johnny Armstrong of Gilnockie in particular. It is said that during the days of James I (r.1513–42) he levied blackmail (i.e. protection money) on certain folk as far south as Newcastle.

The traveller and naturalist Thomas Pennant (1726–98), in his *Tours of Scotland*, noted a curious local superstition from Langholm. In the days before the development of psychology, it was noted that at childbirth the father can suffer along with the mother. Anthropologists have recorded many instances of the custom of *couvade* in which the father takes to his bed and behaves as though he were approaching parturition. A mythical origin of this is traced to Irish legend wherein the wife of Crunnic was forced to run a race against horses while pregnant; and at the end of the race she gave birth to twins. In her travail she cursed all men to suffer the pains of childbirth for nine generations.

Scottish superstition said that a woman's birth pains could be transferred to a man should they exchange clothes just before the birth took place. In 1772 Thomas Pennant wrote of the Langholm midwives having 'the power of transferring part of the primeval curse bestowed upon our first great mother from the good wife to her husband. I saw the reputed offspring of such a labour, who kindly came into the world without giving the mother the least uneasiness, while the poor husband was roaring in agony and in uncouth and unnatural pains'.

Langton, Berwickshire, Borders   CURSE

The old couplet offered grave warning:

> *If ye pass owre the Corneysyke*
> *The corbies will get your banes to pyke*   crows/pick

and folk pointed out 'Bawtie's Grave', near the farm of Broomhouse, as a caution not to thwart the old superstition that said that no human could cross the waters of the Corneysyke Burn by hunt or chase and live.

'Bawtie' was the local rendering from the name of Sieur

Antoine d'Arcies de la Bauté, who was appointed by the Scots Governor John Stewart, Duke of Albany, as Warden of the East and Middle Marches. The Frenchman was appointed in place of Alexander, Lord Home, who was executed in 1516. The peer's kinsmen, the Homes of Wedderburn, swore revenge on the slighting of their family by the elevation of a foreigner and on 9 September 1517 they met up with de la Bauté at Fogo village. He managed to slip from their grasp and took refuge for a while at Langton Tower, and galloped from there when he thought the coast was clear to his base at Dunbar Castle. The Homes, however, caught up with him near Broomhouse and, the old folk recounted, the curse of the burn overtook him. The Homes slew de la Bauté and displayed his severed head on Duns mercat cross.

Largo, Fife   TREASURE

In 1819 a Bronze Age tumulus was found at Norrie's Law with a hoard of seventh-century native Pictish and late Roman silverware. Local folklore has it that a local pedlar called Forbes had some, now unfathomable, access to the silverware and sold a portion of it to a Cupar jeweller called Robert Robertson.

Robertson was later to aver that the hoard had once included a set of silver armour which had been melted down too, yet two silver pieces did survive, a hand-pin and a silver plate which came into the possession of the Society of Antiquaries of Scotland in 1864.

Norrie's Law tumulus lies some two-and-a-half miles north-west of Largo and is so named after a cowherd from nearby Balmain farm called Tammie Norrie who tended sheep and cattle from here to Largo Law. He was known for the strong flourishes he blew on his cattle horn and the stories that he told of how Largo was so full of gold 'when sheep lay on it their fleece turns yellow'. In connection with the folklore of the place is this rhyme:

If Auchindownie cock disna craw
And Balmain's horn disna blaw,

I'll tell you where the gold mine is
on Largo Law.
Woe to the man that blew the horn
For out of the spot he shall ne'er be borne.

Leith, Lothian   FAIRYLORE

Leith began as a small cluster of huts at the side of the Water
of Leith and developed as a port famed for its commerce and
industry. In folklore it can offer a curious fairy tale which was
recounted by the English demonologist Richard Bovet
(b.1641) in his *Pandaemonium, or the Devil's Cloister* (1684).

The story concerns the Fairy Boy of Leith who was
encountered by Captain George Burton, whose account is
reproduced in Bovet's book. The Fairy Boy was about ten
years old when Burton met him and he had a remarkable gift
for telling the future with great accuracy; a gift folk said that
was given to him by the fairies. The boy told Captain Burton
that every Thursday night he went to Edinburgh's Calton
Hill and there entered a complex of subterranean passages
through a secret gate which only he could see because of his
fairy gift. There he would hone his skills in telling the future
and take part in fairy revelry.

The boy described how he beat a drum while the fairy
folk danced and 'A great company, both men and women'
congregated to be amused 'with many sorts of music' as they
ate and drank. Often they all flew off to the Netherlands or
France 'to enjoy the pleasures of these countries', and be back
in a night.

Captain Burton was determined to discover the boy's
secret location on Calton Hill, and with some friends kept a
watch on the boy's movements each Thursday night. With
great skill the boy always evaded them to refresh his skills in
the hill and to return with new prophecies.

Liberton, Lothian   WELL

To the south of Edinburgh, Liberton is said by some to take
its name from a leper colony once served by the nuns of the

medieval convent of St Catherine of Siena.

A central part of the folklore of the place is the Balm Well, an important Scottish medieval healing well which was originally refurbished by King James V in 1517. The well was efficacious in the cure of skin diseases as its waters contain a type of tar from a coal seam at the well's source. Folklore, however, is more flowery in its explanation of the well's powers, and says that the well sprang from a drop of holy oil being transported from the Holy Land, which was accidentally spilled on its way to Queen Margaret, the eleventh-century Queen of Scotland.

Linton, Roxburghshire, Borders   FABULOUS BEAST

Above the door of the Norman church of Linton, in north-east Roxburghshire, is a rare tympanum. It celebrates the expertise of Sir John Somerville, courtier of King William I of Scots, bynamed The Lion. Sir John, it is said, was famous for slaying wild and mythical beasts which terrorised the area.

One folktale in particular tells us that the people of Linton were being troubled by a 'fierce worme' which had a lair in the place now called Wormington, or Worm's Glen. Some four yards long, with a head like a venemous snake, the worme would emerge from its lair at dawn and dusk to prey on local cattle and sheep. Attempts by local men to slay the worme with archery and spears were unsuccessful.

The story of the worme reached the ears of John Somerville, then a young man in search of adventure. He decided that he would slay the worme, but having some flair for military tactical matters he elected to observe the worme's habits first. Somerville watched the worme slither from its lair and begin to search for prey. He then spurred his horse towards the worme and observed its reactions. He saw that it would stand transfixed with its mouth open at anything which moved that appeared bigger than itself, and he noted, too, that it could not move backwards but retreated in a wide circle.

For the next few weeks he trained his horse in certain feints and charges, carrying a flaming peat at the end of a special iron lance. When he knew all was ready he sought out the worme once more. The people of Linton took up position on nearby vantage points to watch the sport. The worme appeared and John Somerville charged and while the beast stood gaping he rammed the flaming peat down its throat and choked it. So was Linton rid of the fabulous beast and Sir John, as he was to become, was honoured in the carved tympanum.

Loch Maree, Ross & Cromarty   CULT SITE

Once an arm of the sea, say some geologists, Loch Maree with its eponymous isle, was named after St Maree or Mael-rubha (d.721) the Irish monk from Bangor. Yet his holy hermitage on the isle was merged with Celtic folklore by the seven-teenth-century chroniclers as a place sacred to the Celtic god Mourie. Indeed up to modern times the Irish saint was nicknamed Mourie.

This god demanded his devotees to sacrifice bulls and the chroniclers said bulls were ferried over to the tiny island made sacred by the devotees sprinkling libations of milk. There the cattle were slaughtered for the psychic betterment of the tribes who lived in the neighbouring hills. A version of these rites lived on through the eighteenth century and local records note how they were enacted in minor form in 1836 and 1852 when ailing local folk drank from the isle's spring water for restored health. The cures were more efficacious, the super-stitious said, if the ritual imbibing was done on 25 August, St Maelrubha's Day.

Loch-An-Eilean, Highland   ECHO

An echo, said Scottish folklore, was the voice of a person's alter ego calling from the world yet to be entered (i.e. death). Loch-an-Eilean, with its remains of the castle once the stron-ghold of the vicious and violent Alexander Stewart, Earl of Buchan (c.1343–1405), nicknamed the 'Wolf of Badenoch', has a triple echo of the 'Wolf' mimicking all who shout out.

Lochaber, Inverness FABULOUS BEAST

In the wild country of Lochaber they still tell the tale of the blacksmith who captured a *glaistig*, the evil Highland spirit that appeared as half-woman and half-goat. Once under lock and key, he knew that the creature would have to offer a gift to be released, as the old superstition recounted. The blacksmith asked for a herd of fine cattle.

Logierait, Tayside HAUNTING

Victorian folklorists dubbed it 'The Most Haunted House in Scotland'. They were referring to Ballechin House on the River Tay in Logierait parish, Perthshire, whose story became a folkloric cause célèbre. The hauntings manifested themselves as a series of sounds like a 'large animal throwing itself violently against the bottom of [a room] door', of rappings, of small explosions and the shrieking of a human voice. The ghostly sounds seemed to have begun after the death of the eccentric, dog-loving former owner Major Robert Steuart (1806–76) and his housekeeper (and some said mistress) Miss Sarah Nicholson (1846–73). The hauntings were to feature in corres-pondence in *The Times* and a famous ghost hunt by the psychic investigator and folklorist Ada Monica Goodrich-Freer (1857–1931); she was to be co-author of a book on the haunting with the wealthy landowner John Patrick Crichton-Stuart (1847–1900), 3rd Marquess of Bute, Rector of St Andrews University.

A regeneration of the hauntings had been witnessed by the Jesuit Father Patrick Hayden who had stayed at Ballechin in 1892; he both heard the strange noises and had seen the apparition of a brown crucifix hovering in his bedroom. Several visitors to the house reported ghostly occurrences that hastened their departure including the family of Joseph R. Heaven who had rented the house and left in terror long before their lease expired. In 1896 visitors to the house began to record seeing a 'hunched backed figure', a 'grey lady' and 'a man with bronzed complexion', and guests reported their beds being shaken violently and the bedclothes torn off as they slept.

In 1897 the Society of Psychical Research made an investigation of the hauntings, funded by Lord Bute, and conducted in the field by Miss Goodrich-Freer, Miss Constance Moore and Colonel G.L. le Mesurier Taylor. During their tenancy a whole range of distinguished 'ghost hunters' were invited to witness the phenomena including the distinguished scientist Professor (later Sir) Oliver Lodge (1851–1940) and physician and psychologist Sir James Crichton-Browne (1840–1938). None is recorded as having 'seen' anything of a psychic nature, except a few extraneous noises, but Miss Goodrich-Freer added to the date of sightings by seeing a 'gliding nun' at the house whom she identified as Ishbel.

The investigations had made no real attempt to ascertain the sources of the 'ghostly sounds', so the whole remained unresolved. One explanation taken up by many was that of seismologist Professor John Milne (1859–1913), who averred that the noises and shakings at Ballechin could be attributed to earthquakes. He opined that the house was in the 'earthquake triangle' made by Pitlochry, Dunkeld and Aberfeldy which all had a history of earth tremors. In due course the chief investigators fell out about the reasons why Ballechin House might have been haunted, but still today the house is remembered as one of the most prominent in the folklore of Scottish ghosts.

M

Maryburgh, Dingwall, Ross & Cromarty

BRAHAN SEER

The folklore of the 'second sight' (the ability to see into the future) had a popular hero in Coinneach Odhar, the Brahan Seer, who worked on the Brahan Estate, Maryburgh, near Dingwall. Born at Uig, Lewis, in the early 1700s, the Seer was as celebrated as Thomas the Rhymer (see pp. 27–30), and like 'True Thomas' his expertise was considered a gift of the fairy folk. His reception of the gift has been told in a number of ways of which this is a distillation: One day Coinneach was cutting peats on the estate and lay down for a while to rest. On waking from a light doze, he found a holed pebble on his chest. Now, Highland superstition recounts that those who have the second sight can look through such a hole and see great prophecies, so Coinneach put the stone up to his eye, and behold, he saw many curious things ... people dressed in strange clothes and locations he thought he recognised but seemed to have grown – villages into towns and tracks into busy roads.

As time went by Coinneach became famed for his prophecies and they began to be written down. One such is said to relate to the Battle of Culloden in 1746. Coinneach had once 'passed over Drumossie Moor (the site of the battle) and had foretold that before many generations had passed, the ground would be stained with the blood of the best of the Highlands'. At the time those who heard his prophecy were puzzled at what it might mean, but as history unfolded the slaughter of Charles Edward Stuart's army seemed to fit the foretelling.

Above Inverness stands the oval hill of *Tom-na-hurich* ('The Hill of the Fairies'). It appears in the Brahan Seer's prophecies as a vantage point from where 'ships would one day be seen sailing round the back of the hill', and 'that the souls of the dead would be sealed in the hillside in the care of the fairies'. The former part of the prophecy was deemed to be fulfilled when the Caledonian Canal was completed in 1847. As to the second, a cemetery was constructed here in 1860.

As with other folkloric personages, Coinneach Odhar, or Kenneth Mackenzie, is likely to have been an amalgam of more than one man in a biographic-folkloric mishmash; his end is linked with Kenneth Mackenzie, 3rd Earl of Seaforth and his wife Countess Isabel, yet as the 3rd Earl died before Coinneach (or, Kenneth) was deemed born, the story is likely to have been attached to someone else of the same name who foretold great events. However, the story goes that the earl went off to France and while he was away his countess invited Kenneth to Brahan Castle (the seat of the Mackenzie chief, beside the River Conon) and asked him what kept her lord in France. At first the seer was reluctant to say, but when pressed said that he could see the earl dallying with a French beauty. The seer fell foul of the countess's wrath and she accused him of witchcraft.

The seer was condemned to death by fire, but before he died he foretold the fate of several Seaforth earls, both in terms of career, misfortune and disability, and as he went to meet his fate he threw his holed stone of prophecy into a loch.

Manor, Peeblesshire, Borders

A few miles south-west of Peebles, in the valley of the Manor Water, lies Kirkton Manor and its surrounding district made famous by one of the most curious figures in Scottish folklore and literature.

Everyone said that David Ritchie came from 'the Devil's territory' under the hills, but Sir Walter Scott mocked that as just superstition; even so Ritchie frightened him, so great was the writer's respect for the supernatural.

Scott was much taken with the academic study of witchcraft – Border superstition in particular – and demonology. Had this not been so, he would never have sought out 'Bowed Davie o' Woodus'. For weeks after his meeting with Ritchie, Sir Walter admitted that 'my flesh crept whenever I stepped out of the brave light of a room into the coweard dark night'.

In August 1797, Scott set out for a tour of the English Lakes with his second elder brother, John, and Adam Ferguson, son of Professor Adam Ferguson, the historian and philosopher. For a time en route they stopped at Professor Ferguson's house, Hallyards, in the Vale of Manor. While at Hallyards, Scott and young Ferguson visited 'Bowed Davie' at his cottage in the Manor valley about a mile fom Hallyards, where, incidentally there is now a statue of him.

David Ritchie was a misanthrope who avoided people. It was hardly surprising. In those unenlightened times his deformities had been subject to ridicule and he had fled from his job as brush maker in Edinburgh to the then remote Borders, where Sir James Nasmyth of Posso had let him lodge. It was perhaps Scott's own lameness (from infantile paralysis) which qualified him as a visitor. Ritchie made Scott and Ferguson stoop through his three-and-a-half-foot-high front door into a low dark room, which became eerie when he drew the rusty bolt. In the darkness Scott could see the squalor in which Ritchie lived, but there were piles of learned books here among the debris of meals. Among the cobwebs and tiny furniture were pots of prepared herbs, dried flowers, sacks of meal and a supply of Ritchie's one luxury – snuff.

Suddenly Walter Scott's blood froze as the dwarf's strangely cold claw-like hand gripped his wrist: 'Man, hae ye ony poo'er?'– magical power. Scott shook his head speechless. At the far end of the room a huge black cat leaped, scattering clattering bowls, into the deep window-hole, and stood with arched back silhouetted against the light. '*He* has poo'er', nodded Ritchie.

Nothing more was said and, half-bewitched, Scott and Ferguson sat on stools, while Ritchie fixed them with his black gleaming eyes. After some minutes Ferguson plucked up courage to ask Ritchie to open the door. They stumbled out into the light. The encounter was attested by John Gibson Lockhart, Scott's son-in-law, in *Memories of Sir Walter Scott*.

Scott's meeting with David Ritchie haunted him for years. He gathered biographical material on Ritchie and eventually he appeared as a character in Scott's tale *The Black Dwarf* (1816). In the book, which was one of Scott's failures, Ritchie appears as Elshie, the dwarf of Mucklestane Moore. In time Scott admitted that his tale, a piece of Gothic extravagance, was poor, but with a certain vanity he half-believed that the book was 'jinxed' by Ritchie who was dead (aged seventy in 1811) before the book appeared.

David Ritchie's cottage, garden and haunts are now a folkloric tourist attraction. The publishers W. & R. Chambers erected a headstone over his grave at Manor churchyard in 1845, and it still offers a curious bit of Border lore. Very superstitious, David Ritchie had a rowan tree planted on his grave to keep the witches away. The rowan, or mountain ash, was long credited as a 'wicken-tree', one which had the power of averting witchcraft, fairies, disease and the ubiquitous 'Evil

Eye'. For, once, this rhyme was readily on the tongue of Borderers:

Rowan tree and red thread
Gar the witches tyne their speed.　　　　　makes/lose

Alas, the rowan did not keep grave-diggers away and when his sister was interred in the same grave in 1821 Davie's deformed bones were removed as a medical curiosity. Even after the failure of *The Black Dwarf*, Sir Walter Scott took no chances. Even though he knew it was ridiculous, he never failed to carry a splinter of rowan in his pocket when he ventured from the calm safety of his study at Abbotsford.

Minto, Roxburghshire, Borders　　　　　UNDEAD

About a mile and a half through Denholm, across the Teviot and flanked by the Minto Hills, Minto House (now demolished) had a busy history, from being a sixteenth-century tower house to emerging as a Georgian mansion and hospital. One owner of the revamped house, Gilbert Elliot, 1st Earl of Minto (1751–1814), died in India, where he had been Governor General. For decades after his death the local folk would never accept that he was dead (even though he was buried at Westminster Abbey). Sir Walter Scott wrote this about the story in 1825:

They think he had done something in India which he would
not answer for – that the house was rebuilt on a scale
unusually large to give him a suite of secret apartments,
and that he often walks about the woods and crags of Minto
at night, with a white nightcap and a long white beard.

N

New Deer, Grampian　　　　　SECRET SOCIETY

Six miles west of Old Deer, where St Columba founded a monastery in the sixth century in which the *Book of Deer* was written as the earliest example of Scottish Gaelic writing, New Deer became famous in folkloric history for a secret society. It flourished for some time at the Whitehill Mill and was a society loosely associated with witchcraft. The members met by night at the miller's kiln to learn the 'tricks of the craft' under the supervision of the miller.

Millers were always popularly associated in Aberdeenshire with witches and the demon of the mill – the 'Kiln Carle' – was the Devil's representative they petitioned as its dwelling in the mill's 'Logie' (ventilation funnel). One leader of the Whitehill Society was miller John Frazer who was said to be a skilled worker of magic. His mill worked when there was no water for the wheels to turn the grinding stones as testimony to his powers. He could also 'reist' (arrest the motion) of the mill so that no one could work it but he; this he did, folks said, to thwart the fairies who would come by night to try to use the mill for their own purposes. Millers in Aberdeenshire, too, were thought to be able to stop and start machinery with the glance of an eye, or the inflection of the voice; thus the power of the 'Miller's Word' was a potent as the 'Horseman's Word'. As many millers kept their mills working on the Sabbath with no interference from local ministers, this led to them being considered men of respected independence.

North Ballachulish, Inverness

Once North Ballachulish and Ballachulish were linked by a ferry across Loch Leven which contains the Isle of St Munda, the canonised Scottish tenth-century abbot who founded several monastic houses in Argyll. The isle, with its ancient burial-places, paved with gravestones, and the surrounding countryside, was an emotive location full of folktale, myth and mystery. Here lies Chief McIan of the Macdonalds, slaughtered at Glencoe on 13 February 1692, and a monument near the Ballachulish Hotel recalls where James Stewart of the Glens (purported assassin of Colin Campbell of Glenure) was hanged in 1752 to stimulate the lore of the 'Appin Murder'.

Folklore also identifies the name of another Highlander in Sir Ewan Cameron of Lochiel (1629–1719). It seems that one day, on the old track leading to the North Ballachulish ferry, that Lochiel was overtaken by the *cailleach* (old woman) benamed Gormul, who was a renowned local witch. When he spied her, Lochiel spurred his horse towards the ferry. But she called after him:

> *'My blessings on you, Ewan Lochiel.'*
> *Your blessings be on yon grey stone, hag,' he ungallantly*
> *replied.*

whereupon the stone was split in two and can still be seen at the north side of Loch Leven.

Many a tale of witchcraft came out of the area around Ballachulish, and these were encouraged when a five-foot-tall figure of a *cailleach* was once found by the ferry site. It had been buried alongside a wickerwork shrine (possibly of Druidic date) and is now in the collection of the National Museums of Scotland.

North Berwick, Lothian   WITCHLORE

A royal burgh, flanking the Firth of Forth, North Berwick was once famous in Scottish folklore for its association with the history of witchcraft and records show two main witch trials here in 1630 and 1663. They were to be minor affairs, though, compared to the events of 1590–93.

The deeds of the North Berwick Witches were recounted in the book *News from Scotland* (1591), which traced the beginnings of the witchlore to a series of miraculous medical cures conducted by a servant woman. In all, these were to lead to confessions under torture, accusations and counter accusations and the involvement of over three score people, including Francis Stewart, 5th Earl of Bothwell (d.1624), charged with high treason.

David Seaton, deputy-bailiff of Tranent, became suspicious concerning the activities of his servant Geillis Duncan. She slipped away from his household regularly as her reputation grew amongst the local folk as a skilled curer of a multitude of ills.

A religious bigot of the Reformed faith and a keen hunter of subversives against the government, Seaton looked upon the girl's skills in herbal remedies as 'unnatural and devilish'. The *News* volume confirms that Seaton tortured the girl into confessing being taken, by 'the wicked allurements and enticements of the devil'.

Turned over to the local authorities, the terrorised girl was compelled to name supposed 'accomplices'. Amongst them were four who were to be brought to trial, and all were of faith and opinions that went contrary to Seaton and his colleagues' beliefs. They included the elderly, blue-stocking Agnes Sampson, the Saltpans teacher Dr John Fian, and two society women Dame Euphemia Maclean, Mrs Moxcrop, daughter of Lord Cliftonhall and Barbara Napier, sister-in-law of the laird of Carschogill.

A prominent player in the dreadful examination of the case was King James VI (1566–1625) whose credulity made him a dedicated believer in witchcraft. The king oversaw the interrogation of Agnes Sampson at Holyrood Palace. After hideous tortures the gentlewoman 'confessed' to fifty-three indictments of witchcraft including trying to capsize the vessel that the king was travelling in en route to Norway to meet his new bride, Anne of Denmark. In time the king was to add to the Scottish folklore library with his *Daemonologie* of 1597.

From the 'evidence' of the four main accused came a recitation of all the accepted witch delusion superstitions – witches flying through the air, the use of toad venom to poison clothes, black cats as familiars, raising storms and honouring the Devil – but dance and music were made much of by the prosecutors. The new faith hardliners looked upon dance as devilish practice, so it was easy for some to believe that the supposed witches had danced around North Berwick church on All Hallows Eve, 1590, and Seaton's servant Geillis confessed to providing music for the witch revellers with her jew's harp as they sang the strange folk rhyme:

Cummer, go ye before
Cummer, go ye;
If ye will not go before
Cummer, let me.

Confessions too, were recorded that at Prestonpans, the North Berwick witches burned a wax image of the king at the behest of Lord Bothwell.

Fian, Sampson and Maclean were all executed by fire, while Napier was released. Bothwell was arrested too because of his erratic behaviour against the king. The crown prosecutors tried to link him with the North Berwick accused – many of them having been his friends and acquaintances – but their case of treason and witchcraft against him failed. Bothwell was released, but ever after was pointed out as the 'Devil of North Berwick'. He died in exile and there were few who did not believe gossip that he practised the black arts to the end.

O

Oban, Strathclyde

FOLLIES/GROTTOES

On the east side of Oban Bay is the *Clach a' Choin* known as the 'Dog Stone', said to have been associated with the folk hero Fingal's dog. Local folklore can add another stone structure that has found particular fame in the lore of follies and grottoes, namely McCaig's Tower. It was built high on a hill in Oban to mimic Rome's Colosseum. It was initiated as a project in 1897 by a local banker to relieve local unemployment, to act as a family memorial and later to be turned into a museum. The project was never completed after the banker died.

Set up in the gardens of stately homes, in the grounds of castles and on hilltops, Scotland's follies and grottoes stand as examples of mankind's eccentric ingenuity. Superlative and stranger than any elsewhere, Scotland's follies and grottoes open up a new chapter of the country's folklore.

A folly is a useless building erected for ornament on a private estate, while a grotto is a pleasant rocky cave which might be quite natural or artificial. The artificial ones are often made of rocks brought to a garden and then decorated with shells. They were usually built by the rich; men like John Murray, 3rd Duke of Atholl (1729–74), who sold the sovereignty of the Isle of Man to the British government. He built a curious fort-like building on his estates called 'The Whim' in 1762.

Follies were built purely for pleasure and for the eccentric tastes of the owners. Folklore has often invested in these places something of the curious spirit (or ghost) of the owner. The great heyday of the folly was the eighteenth century, and ideas for them often came from foreign travel. Many are made, quite cheaply, from local materials, but most evolved in spirit from the romantic poetry and painting of the period.

Follies can include monuments to remembered battles, like the tapering hexagon with pyramidal roof set up in 1911 to commemorate the Battle of Harelaw Hill, Aberdeenshire, in 1411. Some are to people, like the triangular stone to Major-General William Roy (1726–90) – known as the 'Father of the Ordnance Survey' at Carluke, Lanarkshire.

Stirlingshire seems to have more follies than any other Scots county. There's Ossian's Hall on the rocks at Dunkeld, Perthshire; this is a very picturesque folly built in 1758 and restored in 1952. It is set above the wooded gorge of the River Bran. A great area for nature walks, the folly is also known as The Hermitage. Then there is the tower on Kinnoull Hill, a great eye-catcher above the River Tay.

Perhaps the most stupendous Scottish folly is that at Dunmore Park, Stirlingshire. This is in the shape of a pineapple and was built in 1761 as the focal point of the garden. The pineapple was long a symbol of luxury from its introduction. When they were an uncommon fruit in Britain the wealthy could hire them at a guinea (£1.05) as a table display.

Ochils, Central & Tayside   WITCHLORE

With a stretch across the old counties of Clackmannan, Kinross and Perthshire, the Ochil Hills run in an unbroken skein for twenty-four miles. The profuse burns, pools, tracks and wooded land have long been mentioned as places for witch covens. The old maps reflected this superstition in such names as Carlin's Craig, Warlock Glen, Devil's Loch and Deil's Bucket in the region most associated with witches around Logie and Blairlogie. On the River Devon by Rumbling Bridge there's the Devil's Mill, a channel of the river which forms a waterfall which mimics the clattering of a mill wheel – it was so named because 'it never rests on a Sunday'.

Charles Rogers (1825–90), folklorist and antiquarian and editor of the short-lived *Stirling Gazette,* wrote in 1851 that local folk remembered many 'ill-favoured old women' who were deemed to have the skills of witchcraft. Indeed the most often mentioned witch trial at Logie was that of Bessie Finlaysoun on 16 July 1618. During 1658 Black Kate of Parsons-Ley and Auld Meg of Auchintrool were arraigned for witch-inspired murders at Grange, Tulliebody and Clackmannan. At Crook of Devon in 1662 a coven of eleven witches was executed, and the Ochils witchlore was even reflected in local verses:

> *In Quarry Burn, the witches meet, syne through the air,*
> *They scour fu'fleet, they flee, and they flee.*
> *Till they reach Lochy Faulds*   [in Glen Gloom]
> *Whaur Auld Nick in person*
> *His tribunal holds.*

Old Deer, Aberdeenshire, Grampian   TREASURE

The Grey Stane of Corticram marks the place where local folklore says a treasure hunter was crushed to death by its massive hulk while digging at its foot for a pot of gold. A curious local rhyme notes that the only person who could ever be able to locate the gold safely would be borne by caesarean section:

> *The man who never has been born*
> *But from his mother's side been shorn*
> *Sall fynd the plate and golden horn*
> *Anaith the stane o' Corticram*

Lying north of Stronsay, the Isle of Sanday was long a haven on stormy days for the Norsemen's longships. Around their campfires as they sheltered, they spoke of their culture hero Loki, the malicious Merlin of Nordic myth, whose magic spells were long remembered.

When Christianity came to Orkney, Loki was transformed into the Christian Devil. At the ruined Kirk of Lady, near Overbister, five lichen-encrusted parallel grooves in a parapet are pointed out as the Devil's Fingerprints, so wrought in frustration, it is said, when the Devil could not convert the Christian souls of those who worshipped therein to his own ways.

At Broughtown, Overbister, they remember how Loki's book of spells developed in folk memory as *The Book of the Black Arts.* Local credence has it that the book was passed down the generations, for the contemporary owner of the volume of recipes and curses had to dispose of it before death, or the Devil would return to claim the book and the possessor's soul. It seems you could never destroy the book; one girl tried by hurling it into the sea, but on returning home she found the book dry and undamaged by her bedside. Yet, in the nineteenth century, local gossip had it, a clergyman took possession of the book and it is said he owned it up to his death in 1903. Whether he managed to pass the book on, or whether it fell into the hands of the Devil along with his holy soul, none could tell.

Oxnam, Borders   DROVERS

Lying south of Jedburgh, Oxnam leads to what was once the remote upper valley of the Kale Water. An old drove road runs across these hills made up of a remaining part of the Roman road called Dere Street. It was a favourite route for the colourful, characterful drovers who moved the Highland cattle to the English markets (trysts). At one time the droving of cattle from Scotland to England was subject to tax, so secret routes were sought through the Border hills. The drovers were very knowledgeable about the lore relating to cattle; they forecast omens of life and death and the weather by cattle movements and were skilled in treating cattle disease by 'nature magic' (i.e. using herbs and plants collected along the way).

P

Pittenweem, Fife

The Augustinian Priory of Pittenweem was one of the most prominent in medieval Scotland. In the garden of the Prior's house there was a plot long known as 'Witches' Corner', where the cadavers of witch suspects were buried, yet the Augustinian canons had long gone when the burgh became celebrated for its purging of witches.

Records show that Pittenweem had witch trials in 1643 and 1644, but it was that of 1704–05 which gave the ancient fishing port its place in Scotland's witch history. In truth there were no executions for witchcraft at this time, but the two accused died as a consequence of witch hysteria and a third was banished.

The central character of the troubles was one Patrick Morton. Born in 1688, Morton was a teenager at the time of the accusations; he was to prove to be an impressionable lad indoctrinated in witch superstition by the local kirk minister.

During 1704 Morton was an employee at his father's forge, and one day he was directed to forge nails for the wife of a former burgh treasurer of Pittenweem, Beatrix Laing. It seems that Mrs Laing was enraged that the young smith was unable to forge her the nails right away, and she had stalked away in disgust threatening him with some kind of retribution.

Next morning Morton saw Mrs Laing throwing hot ashes from her grate into a tub of water 'and knew his fate was being determined by witchcraft', for such an act had been described to him by the minister. Soon after Morton was 'seized with weakness in his limbs; he lost his appetite and became emaciated'. As 1704 progressed Morton exhibited epileptic fits and other bodily spasms. In his torments he named Beatrix Laing a witch, as well as neighbours Mrs Nicholas Lawson, Thomas Brown, Janet Corphat and others.

Morton became more and more hysterical and more outrageous in his assertions, accusing the women of being disciples of the Devil, who had even come to him to urge him to deny the 'Saviour's name'. Prompted by the local minister, the burgh elders obtained a petition of the Privy Council on 13 June 1704 to detain the accused on a charge of witchcraft. Despite her prominent position in the town, Mrs Laing was seized, tortured and locked up in the town jail. Although retracting it later, she testified against Janet Corphat, Isobel Adam, Mrs Nicholas Lawson and others.

Some of the more temperate members of the burgh authorities reassessed Morton's ramblings and the minister's rantings and Beatrix Laing was freed with a fine. However, she was declared anathema and was banished to St Andrews where she died shunned. One of the accused, Thomas Brown, was starved to death in Pittenweem prison, and the death tally was to be increased to two with Janet Corphat.

Writing in 1871 Thomas George Stevenson declared: 'In places where the minister was inflamed with a holy zeal against the Devil and his emissaries [such as Pittenweem], the parish became a perfect hotbed for the rearing of witches; and so plentiful a crop did it produce, that it appeared nothing else could thrive. But in places where the minister had some portion of humanity, and a little common sense, the Devil rarely set foot on his territory, and witchcraft was not to be found'. In this case the minister was not satisfied that the roots of witchcraft had been severed. Janet Corphat was in jail. Incited by the minister, a mob broke into the prison on 30 January 1705, seized Janet Corphat, beat her and dragged her down to the beach. There she was beaten again and crushed to death under an old door piled up with rocks. 'And to be sure,' wrote Stevenson, 'it was so, they called a man with a horse and sledge and made him drive over her corpse backward and forward several times.'

To their eternal shame the local magistrate and the minister did nothing to prevent the murder of Janet Corphat, so the leaders of the mob went unpunished, and Janet's corpse was flung, as the other dead accused had been, into the communal grave at 'Witches' Corner'.

In due time Patrick Morton was found to be a hysterical impostor. He too was never brought to justice for his wrongful accusations.

Polwarth, Berwickshire, Borders

FOLK HEROINE/CUSTOM

Polwarth Church stands over a burial vault within the old estates of Marchmont House. Within this vault, at the east end of the church, Sir Patrick Hume (1641–1724) hid from the patrols of royalist soldiers in 1685. Hume's name had been mentioned amongst those of the Rye House Plot of 1683 which involved extreme Whigs (Liberals) plotting the assassination of Charles II. For a month Hume lay hidden, fed by his eighteen-year-old daughter – later known as Lady Grizell Baillie (1665–1746) – who brought him food and drink from nearby Redbraes Castle. She kept watch, too, while her father made his way through the estates to safety in his own house, to be concealed under the floorboards until he could flee to Holland. Hume eventually returned, with the Prince of Orange and became 1st Earl of Marchmont in 1697 for his loyal services to the prince, now King William III.

The church is set by the green which still sports two thorns. Around these trees locals would step a marriage dance to ensure fertility for local brides and grooms. The wig-maker-turned-poet Allan Ramsay (1686–1758) remembered the custom in his 'Polwarth on the Green':

If you'll meet me the morn
Where lasses do convene
To dance around the thorn,
A kindly welcome you shall meet
Frae ane that likes to view
A lover and a lad complete,
The lad and lover you.

Q

Queensferry (South), Lothian CUSTOM

A whole list of folklore sources have been advanced for the custom of the Burry Man at South Queensferry, the ancient royal burgh whose name is derived from Margaret, saint and queen of King Malcolm III, bynamed Canmore, who set up a ferry for her journeys from Edinburgh to Dunfermline. Some said he was a fertility symbol from the days of a more rural Scotland, others that he was the representative of Europe's 'Leaf Man' of nature worship. Yet wherever his folklore roots, the Burry Man has been walking the streets of South Queensferry possibly from the day in 1364 when King David II granted the burgh the rights of regality. The Ferry Fair, now held in August and at which he appears, was instituted in 1687. The burrs from the Burry Man's costume come from the burdock plant (Scotland's burr-thistle, *Arctimus bardana*) and this special suit is usually worn by a chosen native of Queensferry; folklore gives to the selected person the name of 'Bellstane Bird'. Covered with burrs from top to toe, and sporting a rose-bedecked hat, the Burry Man processes, supported by two assistants with flower-decorated staves. A circuit is made of South Queensferry's streets with special calls on distinguished locals and visitors.

Once the Burry Man has completed his perambulations the Ferry Fair festivities take place, with races, competitions and events to suit the fashions of the day. A Ferry Queen was first crowned here in 1926.

R

Roslin (Rosslyn), Lothian LEGEND

Once a miner's village, Roslin is set firmly in Scotland's history and folklore for its chapel and castle. Founded *c.*1446 by William St Clair (Sinclair), 3rd Earl of Orkney (d.1480), the chapel was to have been a great collegiate church, dedicated to St Matthew the Apostle. It became the burial place of the Sinclair family and folklore has it that on the night before the death of a member of the family it would be filled with ghostly firelight. As Sir Walter Scott remembers in the *Lay of the Last Minstrel* (1805):

Blazed battlement and pinnet high
Blazed every rose-carved buttress fair –
So still they blaze when fate is night
The lordly line of high St Clair.

The chapel was restored in 1842 by Earl of Rosslyn for services of the Episcopalian rite.

Quite modern folklore particularly cites the 'Prentice Pillar' in the chapel. It is adorned with flower spirals and foliage of great craftsmanship, and it takes its name from the legend that it was carved by an apprentice from a sketch brought back from his travels by Earl Sinclair while his master was away. On his return the master mason is said to have killed the apprentice in a fit of jealous rage. Devotees of the legend point out three carved heads at the chapel's southwest elevation as being of the murdered apprentice, his grieving mother and the master mason.

In recent times folklore about the pillar, and the carvings elsewhere in the chapel, has been expanded. Some aver that the carved plants and leaves are of botany unknown in Britain at that time. Experts have identified them as being of mainland American origin. How could this be when Christopher Columbus's much later voyages to the New World brought back data on the very plants depicted? Even if, as legend says, the pillar was decorated from a drawing brought back by the earl, maybe from Spain or Portugal, no mariner had ventured west from these countries until much later.

So, how did the foliage carvings come to be in the chapel? Some modern folklorists and historians point to the adventures of one remarkable Scots seaman. Henry St Clair was a keen venturer and in 1391 he engaged in the conquest of Frislanda (the Faroe Islands) and met the shipwrecked Venetian voyager Nicolo Zeno. Henry appointed Zeno as the captain of his fleet. Legend goes on that along with Nicolo Zeno's brother, Antonio, Henry St Clair set out to discover a purported rich and populous country in 'the far western sea' of which he had heard from deep-sea fishermen. Henry's fleet set out and was fog-bound and drifted to the west of Ireland from whence they sailed north-westward and discovered Greenland. Henry explored the coast of Greenland for some time and by 1398, the expanded legend said, went to what is now Newport, Rhode Island, North America. It was during this voyage that he came across the botanical specimens that adorn the Rosslyn chapel in relief. Thus Henry St Clair beat Columbus to America.

Rullion Green, Lothian COVENANTER LORE

There are a number of Covenanter Stones in Scotland. They commemorate a group of fanatical Puritan fundamentalists who saw themselves as the Lord's Chosen People. The name 'Covenanters' was given to those signatories of the Scottish National Covenant of 1638 which pledged the upholding of the Presbyterian faith against prelacy and popery. They refused to sign the oath of allegiance at the Restoration of the Monarchy in 1660 and thus became anathema to royalist cadres.

Rullion Green was to be a famous battle in the hagiography of the Covenanters, although they were soundly defeated by General Sir Thomas Dalyell of The Binns (q.v.). A contemporary folk ballad of the day – 28 November 1666 – remembers the poor arms of the Covenanters:

Some had halbards, some had durks
Some had crooked swords like Turks;
Some had slings and some had flails
Knit with eels and oxen tails.

Some had spears and some had pikes,
Some had spades which delvyt dykes;   dug walls
Some had guns with rusty ratches,
Some had fiery peats for matches.

The famous Covenanters' Stone of Rullion Green bears this inscription:

Here and near to this Place lys the Reverend Mr John Crookshanks and Mr. Andrew McCormack Ministers of the Gospel, and about fifty other True Covenanted Presbyterians who were killed in this Place in their own Innocent Self Defence and Defence of the Covenanted Work of Reformation ... Erected Sept 28, 1738.

Ruthwell, Dumfries & Galloway STONE

Now set within an annexe of the church of Ruthwell, the eighteen-foot-high cross, known as the Ruthwell Cross, dates from the late seventh century and is one of the major cult monuments of Dark Age Europe. Its main faces have figure sculp-ture of mostly scriptural scenes with associate Latin inscriptions, and on the sides are rich vine scrolls with birds and beasts long associated with early tribal folklore. On the margins, too, are inscribed in runes (letters of the ancient futhork alphabet), portions of the famous Old English poem *The Dream of the Rood* (a reverie by the execution cross of Christ's death) ascribed by some to the seventh century scriptural poet Caedmon.

S

St Andrews, Fife GHOST HUNTER

Once the ecclesiastical capital of Scotland, the history of St Andrews was also once the history of Scotland. Its wynds and windswept cliffs have seen some of the most rumbustuous episodes of the nation's history. Here John Knox called down the wrath of God on the medieval church and reformers did to death one of the most famous of all the church's princes – Cardinal David Beaton, Archbishop of St Andrews. The town also supplied one of the foremost of Scotland's more dedicated ghost hunters.

When William T. Linskill was not organising 'howkings'

(diggings) in and around the precincts of the ruined cathedral to look for secret passages, he was chasing spectral leads for his articles and books on the subject. The son of Captain W. Linskill, a Mayor of Tynemouth, and his wife, a daughter of Viscount Valentia, Linskill was born in 1858 and was educated at Jesus College, Cambridge. Brought to St Andrews for holidays, he made his home here in 1897 and steeped himself in the burgh's history and current affairs. Elected to the Town Council he eventually became Dean of Guild, but today he is remembered most for his book *St Andrews Ghost Stories*. Before he died on 22 November 1929, the portly, stentorian Linskill became more and more obsessed with his favourite ghost story 'The White Lady of the Haunted Tower'.

In reality the tower concerned is the square building which forms part of Prior John Hepburn's walls around the ruined cathedral precinct. Containing a vault, chambers and a stone-stepped entrance door, the tower was long the burial chamber of such as the Martines, Lairds of Denbrae. In 1868 the tower's upper room was opened and many coffins and bodies were examined. One was the embalmed cadaver of 'a female [who] had on her hands white leather gloves' thus was inspired Linskill's pursuit of the 'White Lady'.

Linskill collected the local fishermens' tales about the tower – for it was just a stone's throw away from the old Fisher Quarter of St Andrews – and how he said 'people used to run for their lives when passing this tower at night; and the older fisher folk have told me some hair-raising uncanny stories of awesome sounds and sights that had been heard and seen by many at that tower'.

By the 1870s the appearance of the spectral White Lady was a common enough occurrence seen by many both walking in the cathedral precincts and on the walls themselves. Linskill collected all the known sightings of the ghost and, in an attempt to tie-in the stories with the 1868 discovery of the white-gloved female's cadaver, he had the tower re-opened at midnight on 21 August 1888. All he found was a jumble of bones, skulls and coffins and no sign of the 'beautiful embalmed girl with the long flowing hair and white gauntlets'. Undeterred, Linskill made the story the centre of his book *The Haunted Tower*. The last sighting of her was by two, apparently sober, medical students in the 1950s.

St Margaret's Hope, South Ronaldsay, Orkney

St Margaret's Hope is where the ship docked carrying Margaret, the Maid of Norway (1286–90). Margaret, daughter of King Eric II of Norway, and granddaughter of King Alexander III of Scotland, was making her way to Scotland for her coronation when she died aboard ship. Her death plunged Scotland into the long wars of Scottish Independence and launched decades of heroic folklore strains of such as Robert I, the Bruce, and the Battle of Bannockburn.

The Horse and Plough Festival was once an Easter tradition at South Ronaldsay, but these days it is held in August. Groups of young people represent 'horses' and 'ploughmen'. Usually girls dress up to be the 'horses' and the customs and grooming are judged in the time-honoured manner. The party then makes it way to the beach for the Boys' Ploughing Match.

Each of the 'ploughmen' has a personal plough, sometimes an heirloom made by a family member, and every participant ploughs a furrow in the sand. Prizes are awarded for skill in ploughing and varieties of plough care and presentation.

Just south of St Margaret's Hope is the village of Burwick. Here is to be found the Ladykirk Stone at St Mary's Church. The stone is marked by two distinctive footprints which folktale says are those of the martyred Orcadian saint Magnus (c. 1076–1116), killed by his cousin Haakon. The saint is said to have sailed across the Pentland Firth on the Ladykirk Stone.

Sanquhar, Dumfries & Galloway

Poldeoch Wood was long associated with fairy folk and locals told the story of how they helped farm labourer Sandy McLachlan. Sandy worked for a mean old curmudgeon called

Farmer Greig and to eke out his meagre wages he would poach a rabbit or pheasant now and again. Greig knew what Sandy was up to and, the story goes, Sandy was poaching when he came across an encampment in the wood. Fairy folk were dancing around their fire and Sandy joined in and became spellbound. Greig swore that he would severely punish Sandy for going missing when he caught up with him. He eventually found Sandy in the wood sleeping peacefully under the fairies' enchantment. Just as he was about to berate him, Greig was surrounded by fairy folk as Sandy awoke. They attacked Greig, and as Francis Merrilees wrote:

> *They climbed upon the farmer's dress*
> *On leggings, boot and gown*
> *And shackled him with spider's web*
> *And Knots of thistledown.*

They emptied Greig's purse into Sandy's lap as back wages and changed:

> *No crop shall prosper, cow shall calve*
> *Nor ewe or lamb shall bear*
> *Till farmer Greig remember he*
> *Most treat McLachlan fair.*

Thus, locals aver, ever after Dumfriesshire farmers were noted for their generosity and respect for their workers.

Scalloway, Shetland NEUGLE

They still point out the black ash on Gallow Hill where local legend has it witches were burned. Yet, Scalloway is more famous in folklore circles as the home of a *neugle*. This beast – from which Scalloway's reservoir, Njugals Water, gets its name – was a Shetland cousin of the better-known water-horse, the kelpie. There are several stories hereabouts of fool-hardy local bravados trying to tame the beast by breaking it as they would a mortal horse; all who tried were carried off beneath the waves of Whiteness Voe.

The Stone of Scone is the most famous of all Scottish historic markers. The traditional story goes that it was brought by Kenneth Mac Alpin (d.858), King of Dalriada, Conqueror of the Picts, to Scone, a prominent Pictish settlement and 'crowning place', and thereafter it was the stone on which Scotland's monarchs were crowned.

Bynamed *Lia Foil* – 'The Stone of Destiny' – a four-teenth-century legend has it that the 26-inch-by-11-inch pinkish-grey sandstone block was the famous Jacob's Pillow of Genesis 28:18: 'And Jacob took the stone that he had put for his pillow and set it up for a pillar. And he called the name of that place Beth-el.'

Tradition averred that it was given to a King of the Celts who married the daughter of an Egyptian pharaoh. To this a sixteenth-century source adds that the stone came to Scotland by way of Egypt, Spain and Ireland to Dunadd, thence Dunstaffnage, Argyll, before it arrived at the Augustinian Priory of Scone.

The generally accepted facts continue that in 1296 King Edward I of England deposed King John Balliol of Scotland and looted the stone from Scone Abbey. But was this the real one? Some say that the Abbot of Scone fobbed off Edward with a replica.

The folklore of the stone was given great publicity when it was removed from the base of the Coronation Chair in Westminster Abbey on Christmas Eve 1950 by disaffected Liberals. The stone reappeared on 11 April 1951 on the site of the high altar of Arbroath Abbey where the grave of King William I (1143–1214), bynamed The Lion, had been. Once repaired the stone was returned to Westminster Abbey.

Modern history has added to the stone's folklore. Some still aver that this returned stone was not the real one either but a late twentieth-century copy, the real one resting in St Columba's Church, Dundee; there it is said to have remained during 1972–89 whence its whereabouts changed, known now only to a few. Nevertheless whatever stone the West-minster one might be, the old prophecy was fulfilled in 1603 with the accession of King James VI of Scotland as James I of England:

If fates go right, where'er this stone is found,
The Scots shall monarchs of the realm be crowned.

Staffa, Inner Hebrides   FOLK HERO

Celebrated for its dark caves, brooding cliffs and visually stun-
ning basaltic pillars and columns, the small uninhabited isle
of Staffa takes its name from the Norse, *staphi-ey,* 'island of
pillars'. It is known particularly for its 227-foot-long 'Fingal's
Cave', immortalised by the composer Felix Mendelssohn
(1809–47) in his *Die Fingals-Höhle* or 'Hebrides' overture
written after his visit of 1829.

In terms of folklore, Staffa is not Norse; it is the territory
of the Celtic folk hero, Fingal, Son of Cumhal, King of the
Tuatha de Danann, the subject of many tales and legends of
Gaelic-speaking Scotland and Ireland (where he is known as
Finn). A warrior-magician, conqueror of giants and monsters,
Fingal is said to have lived in the third century and in folklore
is a hero who led a nomadic life outside the clan system with
his *fian* (war band). In his youth he is said to have been
apprenticed to a magician of the same name who fished for
the salmon of knowledge and wisdom in a pool at the source
of the Boann (Boyne) River; the fish lived off the nuts of the
hazel trees which lined the pool's banks. When the magician
showed Fingal how to fish for the salmon he burned his
thumb on his first catch. On sucking it to relieve the pain
Fingal is said to have become possessed of the magic
knowledge he was to use in his exploits. Like Thomas the
Rhymer and the Brahan Seer, Fingal was to have great
prophetic powers and his magic knowledge gave him the skill
to turn into any animal he wished.

Stories tell of Fingal's exploits against his great enemies
the three Fothads – Aendia (the Single God), Trendia (the
Strong God) and Caendia (the Fair God). Fingal's famous
son was Ossian, after whom the Ossianic cycle of stories is
named. Ossian's mother was said to be the doe called Saar,
and the only outward sign of his cervine origins was a tuft of

fur on his forehead, where his mother had touched him with her tongue.

As to Fingal's place in Staffa, it is said that he used the island as a base in his defence of the Hebrides against sea-raiders.

Stenness, Orkney

Maeshowe Chambered Cairn at Stenness, situated around nine miles fom Kirkwall is considered to be the finest megalithic tomb in Britain. Herein a large mound covers a stone-built passage and large corbelled burial chamber. It dates from Neolithic times at *c.*2000 BC. Folklore has this chamber as the habitation of a *Hogboy* (from the Norse *haugbui*, a ghost). Several of the chamber's walls are carved with Norse runes and there is a clearly carved Viking dragon, taken by the superstitious to be a marker for a hidden treasure.

The Stone of Odin (removed 1814–15) was once an integral part of the folklore of the site. Custom was that on New Year's Day local young people would congregate at the Kirk of Stenness bringing with them food to last for almost a week. Those of the young folk who had agreed to marry then went to the Stones of Stenness (a Bronze Age stone circle on the southern shore of the Loch of Harray) – bynamed locally the 'Temple of the Moon'. Here the young women would kneel before their intended husbands and pray to the god Woden (Odin) 'to perform all the promises and obligations [they were] to make'. Then the couples would walk on to the 'Temple of the Sun' (Bronze Age Ring of Brodgar, north-east of the Loch of Stenness) where the men repeated the women's prayer. At last they would proceed to the Stone of Odin ('Temple of the Stars') where they would clasp hands through the hole bored in the stone. Thus were the intended marriages publicly attested and blessed by the old gods of the place. People suffering from a multitude of diseases would walk (or be carried) three times round the Stones of Stenness for a certain cure, the superstitious assured.

Those interested in Norse folklore can note that just beyond the Kirk of Stenness are the ruins of the House of

Stenness (site of the ancient folkloric *Bu*) where Ragnhild murdered her Viking husband Havard-Jarl in the late ninth century.

Several of the folklore strains of Stenness are used as atmospheric background by Sir Walter Scott in his book *The Pirate* (1822).

Strathpeffer, Highland   HEALING WELL

Once this old Ross & Cromarty town, set near the foot of Ben Wyvis, had a highly reputed spa well where folk came to drink the chalybeate spring water. The so-called healing waters of Strathpeffer were sought out long before the fine folk came from Edinburgh and Glasgow for medicinal cures, as the Pictish relics in the hills around testify.

There are some 600 recorded holy wells in Scotland from Yelaburn, Unst, to Kirkmaiden, Galloway, and from St Kilda's Well of Youth to the Corryvannoch Well in Angus. Originally they would probably have been a part of a shrine to a local deity. One such with a continual history from heathendom to Christianity was that on the island of Eigg which in time was dedicated to St Katherine.

Although many wells were visited on the feast days of the saints to which they were dedicated, in Scotland folk made trips to the wells on Quarter Days, with a fair often being held in the vicinity of the well. Well ritual depended upon the extent of superstition and devotion. Often people walked around the well three times (in the direction of the sun's path – deasil; witches went the other way – widdershins). Some threw in money, others drank the water and wished and left an offering like a pin, a piece of cloth, or flowers and food in race mimic of prehistoric libationary and sacrificial offerings. Usually all well ritual was enacted in silence.

As time went by some wells became more popular than others, like St Mary's Well, Isle of Mull, and the well dedicated to the same saint on the Isle of May, deemed efficacious to barren women. Some wells were thought to cure certain illnesses. St Fillan's Well, Perthshire, was thought to be good for mental troubles, while St Bride's at Pitlochry was sought out for consumption (pulmonary tuberculosis). St Catherine's Well at Liberton was said to cure skin diseases, while St John's Well at Balmanno was one to cure rickets.

Other wells were said to have prophetic powers. The Dripping Well at Avoch, Ross & Cromarty, was one visited in tandem to the Strathpeffer Well; here the Brahan Seer topped up his skills and told others: 'Whoever he be that drink of the water henceforth shall, by placing two pieces of straw or wood on the surface, ascertain whether he recover or not. If he is to recover, the straws will whirl round in opposite directions, but if he is to die soon, they will lie motionless.'

In pre-Reformation times wells were 'dressed' with flowers on certain saints days. At Dunfermline, on 20 July they dress the Holy Well of St Margaret, and there was once not a young lover in the know who did not bring flowers to a holy well on St Valentine's Day (14 February) to secure one's love; Midsummer's Eve was the time to visit a holy well to mend a broken heart. In the days before sophisticated cosmetics Old Beltane Day (1 May) was a good time to visit a holy or healing well to wash the face for enhanced looks. One well in particular, St Anthony's Well, by the ruins of St Anthony's Chapel, Arthur's Seat, Edinburgh was reserved for beauty enhancement cures.

T

Tay (Loch), Tayside

TINKERS

Fed by the rivers of Dochart and Lochay, the salmon-rich fourteen-and-a-half-mile-long Loch Tay was ever a favourite spot for generations of Scots tinkers. They were nomadic, or quasi-nomadic groups of people whose mode of living was like that of the gypsies, although true tinkers have no relationship with gypsies at all.

It is likely that the Scots tinkers socio-cultural group is made up of the descendants of a wandering caste of metalworkers whose skills, within ancient tribal Scotland, gave them status. Many were skilled tinsmiths and were long credited with secret powers for their working with the 'white' metal.

The ranks of Scotland's tinkers were added to at various eras of the country's violent history. Famines, religious wars, and the outcome of such battles as Culloden (1746) and the Highland Clearances led to the swelling of the dispossessed who took to the roads for a living with many merging with the extant tinker clans. In time Scots tinkers evolved their own language – the cant – which varied from the tongue of the tinker-gypsies of Galloway to the *Beurlacheard* ('lingo of the cairds' [tinkers] of the Highland tinkers which is a sort of secret language mixed with archaic Gaelic).

Scots non-tinkers (called 'flatties' by the tinkers) always feared tinkers as child-stealers. Hence the old lullaby:

Hush ye! Hush ye! Dinna fret ye!
The black Tinker wanna get ye.

Yet it is clear that tinkers also feared the flatties. In the nineteenth-century tinker-lore there is reference to a great fear of the 'burkers' (body snatchers so named after the monstrous body-snatcher William Burke who, with his collaborator William Hare, terrorised low-life Edinburgh). As they travelled around Tayside the tinkers kept a watch for the body-snatchers from Edinburgh, Glasgow and Aberdeen who they believed followed the tinker routes to waylay and murder tinkers to sell their cadavers to the medical schools, so the folklore of tinkers is full of stories of 'burkers' and 'noddies' (medical students). The root of this folklore, though, was probably older than the nineteenth-century, for even in seventeenth-century Scotland it was a capital offence to be a tinker, gypsy, vagabond, minstrel or travelling smith with no fixed habitation.

Tinker folklore belief includes the whole gamut of ghosts, witches and kelpies, but most of the stories they retold were about fairies. In Scottish tinker lore, the most famous tinker clan was the MacPhees, who were universally considered bad luck (because of the number of them who fell foul of the law and were executed), so the name 'MacPhee' entered tinker taboo language; should you by accident mention the name you should touch any iron object right away to counter the evil.

Tiree, Inner Hebrides WITCHCRAFT/RONAG

For decades folk came to the low, windswept island of Tiree for the fine pink marble speckled with green. Some took pieces away to fend off the Evil Eye, but on Tiree they had their own way of keeping witches at bay.

It is said the witches of Tiree, and neighbouring Coll and Mull, were adept at stealing milk. To put a stop to their ploys the folk of Tiree would make up a ball of animal or human hair called a *ronag*. This would be placed into a milk pail on Lammas Eve (1 August) and left for twenty-four hours. The charm, the superstitious said, would keep the witches away for a twelve month.

Tullochgorum, Invernesshire PROPHECY

Famed for its inclusion in the title of a Strathspey dance tune, composed by Hamish Dallasach, an eighteenth-century Scottish fiddler, Tullochgorum lies six miles south-west of Granton on the River Spey. The Clan Grant of Freuchie were progenitors of the Tullochgorum Grants and whenever a member of the latter branch was about to die, the giantess known as Mag Moulach would appear waving her long, hairy arms as a warning of the impending demise.

Tummel (Falls of), Tayside BUCKIE

William Shakespeare made the best-known literary reference to the folklore character called Puck in his play *A Midsummer Night's Dream*. In folklore Puck is known as a hobgoblin, a mischievous trickster who could transform one object into another of quite opposite nature; an apple into a kettle, for instance.

The Scots equivalent of Puck was Buckie, and the most famous lair of this folklore character was the Falls of Tummel. From here he would emerge to seek out travellers on the Perth to Inverness road to play tricks on. Highland folk called him Bucan, and in the southern Lowlands he was Boggart, or Bogie, the progenitor of the Victorian Bogie-man.

Wherever he appeared there would be chaos, although on occasions he could show compassion. He seemed to have had a soft spot for millers; and any who fell behind with their milling, or encountered hard times, might expect a visit from the Buckie to help out in a positive way.

As to folk roots of Buckie, local Perthshire lore said he was the child of a fairy king by a mortal woman. In origin though, he is probably a race memory of a minor fertility god or spirit.

Turriff, Grampian

FOLK ANIMAL/
SECRET SOCIETY/DEVIL

Set above the Idoch Water, Turriff has known habitations since at least the seventh century. Once, too, the locals had a healthy respect for the Devil for here were 'Goodman's Crofts' marked as land set aside to serve his needs, but his place in folklore is much more modern and is based on the story of the 'Turra Coo'. During 1913 a local farmer, called Robert Paterson, refused to pay insurance stamps to the Inland Revenue for his workers. The area's Sheriff's Officer seized one of Paterson's cows with the order that the beast should be sold to pay the insurance. The town was in an uproar when the cow's auction took place, and during the proceedings the 'Turra Coo' bolted and was goaded on by fellow farmers sympathetic to Paterson's stance. Eventually the cow was returned to Paterson's farm of Lendrum, and there it lies buried with a granite headstone to remember the story which is now a firm part of Turriff folklore.

There were many so-called Hell-Fire Clubs in the north-east of Scotland well into the 1890s. The members of these clubs 'pledged themselves to the Devils service' and their meetings were an orgy of drunken behaviour and blasphemy. Once a year – in a mock ceremony aping of the Presbyterian Communion service – they celebrated communion in the Devil's name. In this part of the world the Devil was known as the 'Dusky Potentate'. Most members were rebels against the religious strictures of the day as they saw them.

A part of the Hell-Fire Club's activities was drinking a

toast to the Devil. Such a club was extant at Turriff, it is said, for many years, certainly from the seventeenth century. An entry in the presbytery records for Turriff under the date 26 August 1647 'compears' (summons) one Andrew Hogs that he 'confessed yt on the Lord's day, he had drunken the Devil's good health at the Cross of Turriff, confusion to the parsone of Turriff and to the Covenant, and with him John Burnet, Gilbert Harper and Donald MacKedy, pyper, piping to the drink, and Wm Kay who come all from the house of Delgatie'. Later in October of that year, Donald MacKeddie swore to the Presbytery of Turriff that he was 'peied to be piper at ye drinking of ye devell's health at the Cross of Turriff and refused yt he Drank it himself'. Delgatie Castle is northeast of Turriff.

The presbytery records show that these men were much taken with nature worship, and folklorists believe that they were more likely to be re-enacting a race memory of libations to primitive gods rather than as part of a witch coven or satanic group openly worshipping the Devil.

Tweedsmuir, Peeblesshire, Borders   LEGENDS

The region around Tweed's Well, where the River Tweed begins its 97-mile journey to the sea at Berwick-upon-Tweed, is as much a fount of Border Folklore as it is to Scotland's third longest river. The hollow in the hills called Devil's Beef Tub sets the scene and in the town, by Tweedshaws, Merlin is said to have met St Kentigern when King Arthur's warriors fought the men of the hills hereabouts at the Battle of Liddel Valley. Tweedsmuir appears in an old Arthurian story which mentions one of folk nursery's most famous characters.

'Jack the Giant Killer' appears in many European folktales as 'the wise fool', or a young fellow of 'rustic naivety', whose openness brings him rich rewards. The famous story of 'Jack and the Beanstalk' is a favourite variant of the theme. One version set at the time of King Arthur has Jack kill the giant of the Tweedsmuir hills.

The Tweedsmuir giant was called Cormelius who was over eighteen feet tall and he had harried the little hill hamlets for many years. Jack digs a pit outside the giant's cave and covers it over with earth and heather. Then he sounds a challenge to the giant on his horn. Cormelius runs out to see who is challenging him and falls into the pit. Jumping into the pit Jack finishes off the giant with an axe. He is rewarded with the treasure the giant has amassed in his cave.

Jack sets off home up the Tweed Valley and encounters a second giant, who declares that the treasure Jack has is really his. 'Give the treasure to me,' glowered the giant, 'or I'll bash your brains out with my club.' However, Jack challenges the giant to a strange duel. Beneath his coat Jack has a bag of meal concealed. He taunts the giant that he, Jack, is invincible and can plunge a dagger into his flesh and still live; could the giant do the same? Of course he could, the giant boasts. Jack digs his knife into his stomach and only pierces the meal bag. When the giant does the same he kills himself. Thus Jack retains the treasure and goes home safely.

At Tweedsmuir a group of ancient stones were pointed out as the 'Grave of Jack the Giant Killer'.

U

Unst, Shetland   CAIRN/TREASURE

Pictish and Norse folklore roots are to be found at Unst, the northernmost of the Shetland Isles. Folklorist point out a cairn which is deemed to be the burial place of a legendary King Harold of Norway. Unst Haroldswick is said to be named after his invasion. Local tales said that a great treasure was to be found at this Viking site, but an excavation of 1865 discovered none. From time to time superstitious locals have added stones to the cairn whenever they passed by, to ensure that the 'evil creatures' who inhabit the cairn are kept sealed in.

V

Vallay, Outer Hebrides

The two-and-a-half-mile-long island of Vallay, only half a mile away from the north-west coast of Uist, has a folklore phenomenon maybe unique in Scotland.

Locals know the whereabouts of a pit which the superstitious say can never be filled. The reason is that it once sealed the grave of a witch who was buried alive in it for the serious crime on Vallay of stealing milk. The theft of milk (a valuable commodity in a rural community) was a crime often associated with witches, and local folklore said witches accomplished the robbery in a variety of ways. The witch could become a hare and suck the cows dry, or recite spells to empty a pail from a distance. The most bizarre explanation was that the witch stole milk using a magic milking tube.

W

(East) Wemyss, Fife

A castle, estate and three villages all take their names from the numerous *weems* (caves) along the northern coastline of the Firth of Forth, not far from the sixteenth-century Macduff Castle. Each cave still exhibits a variety of inscriptions of interest to the folklorist and social historian from the prehistoric double disc symbols to the graffiti of unfolding ages.

The Court Cave, the Doo Cave, Jonathan's Cave and Sliding Cave – though much desecrated and neglected by decades of both civic and public apathy – show relics of Bronze Age, Pictish and Norse folklore as well as Christian symbols. The caves were often used as hideouts for outlaws, smugglers and gypsies.

(West) Wemyss, Fife

Of all the colourful ghosts of Scotland's spectral pantheon, the 'green ladies' are the most commonly encountered by mortals. They are to be found from Banff to Breadalbane, but one of the most famous is she of Castle Wemyss.

A Burgh of Barony since 1511, West Wemyss was once a prosperous centre of salt-panning, then as a coal port. On the clifftops above the Firth of Forth, Castle Wemyss broods dramatically.

There's been a castle here since around 1420 and at 'The Hall of Wemyss' Mary, Queen of Scots, first met her future husband, the ill-fated Henry Stewart, Lord Darnley. The castle was long said to be haunted by a green-hued ghost, described by a visitor in the 1890s as 'tall and slim and entirely clad in green, with her visage hidden by the hood of her mantle'. She was seen by domestics and family alike, but some curious power always stopped anyone being able to speak to her.

Y

Yarrow (Vale of), Borders   WITCH

The visual beauties of the Vale of Yarrow form one place in Scotland which inspired folksongs and poems by the dozen and quickened the pens of such as Scott, Hogg and Burns. One folklore story from the 'Dowie Dens' [gloomy glens] of Yarrow reminds of witchcraft belief and dates from around the time that James Graham, Marquis of Montrose (1612–50) was defeated by the Covenanters at the nearby Battle of Philiphaugh in 1645.

The story concerned two young blacksmith's apprentices, one of whom was regularly tormented by a witch. The boy related that the witch entered his bedchamber every night and placed a horse's bridle on his head. Instantly the boy was transformed into a horse and the witch galloped off astride him across the Yarrow hills. Learning of his brother's plight, the apprentice's elder brother volunteered to take the boy's place one night and await the witch's coming. At length the witch arrived and transformed the boy into a horse and rode away to her coven in the hills, leaving the boy-horse tethered to a tree. With a mighty toss of the head the horse slipped off the bridle and the boy was re-transformed to a mortal. The boy now waited in hiding for the witch to return. When she did so he threw the bridle over her head and galloped her back to the forge. There he shod the witch-horse and the next day, the folktale goes, she was found in her garden writhing in agony with horseshoes nailed to her feet.

Yester, Lothian   WARLOCK

The village of Gifford was moved in the seventeenth-century to its present site from a location near Yester House, the seat of the Marquis of Tweeddale. Some two miles from Gifford lies the ruin of Yester Castle.

The castle, set on a promontory by Hopes Water and its tributary, legend has it, was built around 1267 by Hugo de Gifford of Yester, benamed the Warlock of Gifford, using a particularly powerful magic spell to summon unseen building hands. The centre-piece of the enchanted site was the sub-terranean vaulted chamber known in local folklore parlance as Goblin Ha [Hall].

Although members of the Scottish fairy realm of Elfhame, the mischievous and impish sprites known as goblins do not feature much in the nation's folklore, being overshadowed by their native cousins the brownies. Hugo of Yester, however, was deemed to have been able to harness their skills to carve a linking part to his chamber (where he worked his magic) out of the natural rock. In his poem 'Marmion', Sir Walter Scott has the hero of the tale seek out of the elfin warrior of 'Goolin Ha' who centuries before had fought with Alexander III. Today a hotel in Gifford reminds of the old folklore by using the name 'Goblin Ha'.

Yetnasteen, Rousay, Orkney   GIANT

Divided from the mainland of Orkney by Eynhallow Sound, Rousay offers the folklorist the giant's stone of Yetnasteen. The stone is invested with the curious power of being able, on New Year's morning, to walk down to the Loch of Scock-ness to drink.

A gory Rousay legend has it that the Giant of Yetnasteen kidnapped three Norse sister princesses. Two he murdered for their skins; the third he kept alive to spin his wool and weave his clothes. At length the girl was able to retrieve her two sisters' skins and by magic restored them to their bodies. Using her charms she persuaded the slow-witted giant to carry down the two girls to the seashore in baskets of grass, without realising what he was doing, and thus they were able to escape back home. The girls duly returned with a longship, and with the help of their mother they scalded the giant to death in a vat of boiling water.

The skins story, of course, mirrors the Orcadian beliefs regarding mermaids sloughing their skins to take on a mortal life.

Z

Zetland (Shetland)　　　　SUPERSTITIONS/TRENDS

Named from the Old Norse *Hjalti's* [Land], Zetland, as the antique cognomen for Shetland, survived in the title of the County Council until 1975, and still as a marquisate of the Dundas family from 1892. Shetland retains a rich and individual folklore with its own interpretations of witches, giants (like Alta of the Scalli Hills), fairylore (trolls/trows), *foys* (feasts) and *Fanteens* (fasts), and the cult of heroes (from King Arthur to Norse gods).

The old Shetlanders were much taken with what they called *vessiks* and *goadiks* (folk rhymes and riddles), some with obvious references to the gods and godesses of the Vikings. Some folk rhymes were used as incantations. Here's one that was recited to secure any object of desire:

Da man o' micht	The man of might
He rod an nicht	He rode all night
We nedder swird	With neither sword
Nor faerd nor licht	No food nor light
He socht da mare	He sought the mare
He fand da mare	He found the mare

He bund da mare	He bound the mare
Wi' his ain hair	With his own hair
An' made her swear	And made her swear
Bi Midder's micht	By Mother's might
At she wid never bide a nicht	That she would never stay a night
Whaur he had rod	Where he had ridden
Dat man o' micht	That man of might.

Many of the riddles were simple couplets:

Lifts ower the heather, sinks idda sea   over/in the
Fire canna burn it, what can it be?   cannot
[*Answer:* The Sun]

Or:

When I gang oot I keep my face to me hame   go out/home
And when I come in me face is frae me hame.   from
[*Answer:* A man in a row boat going to
and from the fishing ground]

The root of these riddles is undoubtedly the ritual patter of the tribal trickster/shamans of previous centuries.

The fisherfolk had their own rich superstitions. Amongst the most superstitious of the Shetland fishermen were those of the *haf* boats. This type of 20-foot fishing vessel died out in the 1880s. For instance on their first night at sea the skipper of such a boat arriving at its fishing location would open the vessel's *buggie* (sheepskin bag) and take out three *biddies* (oatcakes); these he would cut into halves with his special *skone* (sea-knife) and distribute to the crew. The pieces of oatcake were thought to bring a prosperous catch. These fishermen also had their own particular taboo language. Lest they scare off fish (or offend sea creatures) they never used the English language names of them. Thus they referred to *da fish* (or *da glyed shield*) for halibut; *neesak* for porpoises; *skulp* for jellyfish; *knoklins* for mussels and so on.

Shetlanders also had their own fabulous sea creatures.

One such was the *bregali*. This monster would chase fishing boats at sea and those it caught it would crush in a powerful embrace. Others the monster might entwine over the gunwales in its long fins and drag to the bottom. To prevent such a drowning, the master of the vessel had to cut the fins with his sea knife, for everyone knew that the *bregali* did not like steel.

Index